Comp[illegible]ope

Scorpio 2024

Monthly astrological forecasts for 2024

TATIANA BORSCH

Translated from Russian by Sonja Swenson
Translation copyright © Coinflow Limited, Cyprus
AstraArt Books is an imprint of Coinflow limited, Cyprus
Published by Coinflow Limited, Cyprus
For queries please contact: tatianaborsch@yahoo.com

ISBN 978-9925-609-40-6 (paperback)
ISBN 978-9925-609-41-3 (ebook)

Contents

General Astrological Forecast for 2024

We are embarking on yet another difficult year, which can generally be divided into two very different periods. During the first half of the year, Jupiter, which is the most powerful planet in our solar system, will be in the sign of Taurus, creating a favorable aspect with Saturn. That means that both peoples' lives and events on the political stage will play out rather predictably.

This is a very good time for China – it will continue to expand its power, both economically and politically, which will of course impact its position in the global arena. We might see successful negotiations regarding Taiwan.

The first half of 2024 will also be very positive for India. Its economy is surging – over the next three to four years, it will be able to make significant investments in resolving problems such as poverty and develop its infrastructure and industry. It will become a global economic leader.

However, things are not so rosy in the Old World – Europe, where economic drivers such as Germany, are going through a troublesome astrological period. In India, this is known as Sade Sati (Saturn's transit through the sign of the Moon, which often includes the Moon's neighboring zodiac sign). Usually, this period lasts about three years. Each country will experience things its own way. For Germany, this most likely means an economic slowdown and domestic political and social turbulence. This is a trend that began in 2022 and will last for about three years.

The first half of 2024 is crucial for Russia, as presidential elections will take place in 2024. I predict that Putin will remain in power, despite the Russian opposition and meddling from the West, which will be unprecedented this time. Though Putin will remain in the Kremlin, his government will see a lot of turnover, as will other power structures.

The war in Ukraine will begin to slow down somewhat during the first half of the year, and though there will not be any major hostilities, skirmishes will break out in various spots on various fronts.

Ukraine's difficulties began with the Sade Sati in 2020. In 2024-2025, we will see this phenomenon reach its final phase. I believe that there is a very high chance of the country being divided into spheres of influence, with its very independence jeopardized. In 2024, and perhaps somewhat sooner, Poland might openly lay claim to Lviv and the western territories that were ceded to Ukraine following World War Two.

With regard to Ukraine's territories currently under Russian occupation – we will see a continuation of major construction and infrastructure restoration. I believe that in the first half of 2024, Russia's expansion may continue, as other Russian-speaking regions of Ukraine fall under its influence. May 2024 might be a very important time for this.

Economically, this is a hard time for Russia. Sanctions and trade limitations will make things significantly more difficult. There may not be enough budget for military operations, along with economic development, and major construction in the regions now impacted by war. But in the end, there will be an acceptable balance. Russia's economic recovery will be active enough, and as a result, we might see new companies created in regions around the country.

A major astrological event will take place from April 18-26, 2024. Two giants of the solar system – Jupiter and Uranus – will be in conjunction. This is one of the most unusual unions when it comes to finances. Depending on individual horoscopes, some people might see significant achievements here, while others will see unexpected changes for the worse. In principle, this is a neutral-positive aspect, but everything depends on individual information. This is an interesting time for cryptocurrency – we might see significant ups and downs with new financial instruments, which will seriously alter the currency markets, as Uranus in Taurus will lead to many financial shifts.

But also remember that during this time, we may see positive business propositions, career changes, promotions, salary raises, and successful investments!

In 2024, all businesses related to agriculture and produce might develop rapidly. More people might be noticeably more focused on eating a healthy diet.

The second half of 2024 will be much more troublesome for all countries, and far more difficult than the first half.

On May 25, Jupiter will transit to Gemini, and by June, we might start to see changes in plans and conflicts drag out, both in our interpersonal relationships and between countries. By mid-August, Jupiter will be forming a harsh aspect with Saturn, which promises a battle between old structures and the new world we live in. This aspect will repeat again in the fall and winter of 2024. Our world abounds with contradictions, and this will only become more apparent. The economic crisis will worsen, and almost no country will be spared.

The war in Ukraine will gain momentum once again. In the fall and winter of 2024, things will become difficult for Russia, as the hostilities take on a new intensity. This will continue into the first half of 2025, though gradually it will become clear that there is no military solution to this conflict, and things will start to die down. Sanctions will remain in place, though slowly but surely, things will head in a more constructive direction.

During the second half of the year, the European Union will see division among its member states. This trend will continue into 2025 as well. We might see some countries moving toward greater independence from Brussels. The reason may be the economic crisis, which will force many governments to work on behalf of their own countries.

Obviously we won't see any repeats of Brexit in 2024, though this may appear somewhat later. Over the next three to four years, the EU will undergo serious changes, and the European Commission might lose some of its powers, as dictating the rules of the game to the world will become much more difficult.

With regard to the United States, 2024 might be particularly difficult. Pluto is returning to its position in the US birth chart, and this is very important, as it will be in the sector of the sky responsible for the banking system, finances, and even society's emotional state.

Pluto is the planet responsible for purification and renewal, but it also brings the destruction of anything obsolete, which may trigger global crises, which are inevitable with any change in the system. That is why in 2024, economic strife may trigger demonstrations against the current government, as well as a serious struggle for power among members of the ruling class.

During the second half of the year, the United States may lose a lot of allies – this trend will continue into 2025. Perhaps this will be due to a stronger China, Russia, and India, or alternatively, growing economic problems. The US will weaken in its role as the hegemon.

The US presidential elections in 2024 may bring a repeat of what we saw in 2020. It is hard to imagine Joe Biden hanging onto the presidency. He will leave. But these elections will be full of scandal, most likely due to Trump's bombastic speeches.

During the second half of the year, Jupiter will be in Gemini, which supports Trump, as he himself is a Gemini. During the first half of the year, however, despite his histrionics, Trump will spend the first half of 2024 busy with legal troubles that began in 2023. But during the second half of the year, he will be at the center of society's attention – what more could a politician need? Both Trump and Ron de Santis have a good shot at the presidency. De Santis's birth time is unknown, but I think he has a good chance.

Another thorn in the US's side may be the situation in the Middle East, which is already unstable, but in 2024, some kind of military confrontation may break out.

Jupiter in Gemini creates a negative aspect with Saturn, which will close in mid-August, and which portends difficulties for the global economy. This means a situation that is highly unstable, with volatile markets and trouble in the banking sector.

We might, however, see scientific breakthroughs – perhaps new technology and discoveries await in the hands of the world's young and talented scientists.

Fashion will become more feminine and elegant during the first half of the year. Jupiter in Taurus means that we can expect more fitted silhouettes, and perhaps greater focus on traditional garb. Beige will be the color of the day, as will all hues of gold and brown. As always, black will be in demand. Clothing will be monochromatic.

During the second half of the year, we can expect light and dark blue, green, and unusual color combinations. The look will be unkempt and carefree, with a greater focus on youth fashions than the classics. Jupiter in Gemini also suggests flowing, translucent fabrics.

All year long, the weather will be unstable, with flooding affecting coastal countries and islands. We might see a more serious version of what has already happened in several regions of the world. During the second half of the year, many countries can expect to deal with strong winds and tornadoes.

While we can say that everyone has their own fate, global circumstances often are indirectly reflected in each of our lives.

Despite all the ups and downs, the first half of 2024 is the best time for getting married, having babies, or buying real estate.

During the second half of the year, I would not recommend any long-distance travel, starting any legal proceedings, or making important decisions about moving. During this time, many relationships will fall apart, if things were already on the rocks. But you can find out more about that in my forecast for each Zodiac sign.

Best of luck in 2024!

Astrologist Tatiana Borsch

2024 Overview for Scorpio

2024 will bring you new plans, which will then come to life. In the meantime, it is worth considering what you really need and what would be easy to give up.

Work

You will see varying levels of success at work. Many Scorpios will meet someone influential. Business owners and managers will be working on joint cooperation, which will benefit you, but also bring challenges when you run into people who are more influential than you.

Though you can expect to avoid nearly all problems during the first half of the year, during the second, you will run into a series of disagreements.

Perhaps your business partners will start behaving selfishly, which will reflect negatively on your relationship and business in general. Alternatively, he or she might make financial demands or become difficult when it comes to real estate. Perhaps that will take place somewhere far away, or closer to home.

During the second half of the year, employees can expect changes at work, which might continue into 2025. That may force you to adjust to changes in conditions or think about taking your talents to greener pastures. But Rome wasn't built in a day, so take your time in making any decisions and examine all the possibilities before you make a move.

The most difficult period is the second half of the year, especially

December, when the challenges that began in August come at you, full force.

Money

In 2024, your bank account will see a lot of ups and downs. Your income is modest, but you will still have expenses, especially in the second half of the year. They may be related to weak spots in your business, or perhaps your personal life and your family's, or more likely, children's demands.

Love and family

You can expect significant shifts in your personal life. Jupiter, the planet of success, is in the sector of the sky responsible for marriage, love, and any long-term relationship.

Thanks to this, single people and those who have been let down by love in the past, can count on a fateful meeting, which will logically lead to living together or perhaps even marriage.

You can also expect relationship troubles, especially during the second half of the year, with the stormiest clouds gathering from August to December.

In the best-case scenario, this is just part of the normal hiccups we run into when getting to know one another, but in the worst cases, you will realize that your loved one's worldview or values system clashes with your own.

During this time, those with families can expect difficulties involving their children, and these issues may look different, depending on how old your children are, as well as past situations.

Spouses who have been together for a while can count on their loved one significantly strengthening his or her position at work.

Things are not perfect here, though, either – the arrival of someone on the sidelines is a real possibility, and this always makes our life more complicated. Skeletons always come out of the closet one way or another, and during the second half of the year, you will see just how true that is.

Health

In 2024, you will be feeling sluggish, especially from August to December. During this time, old, chronic illnesses may rear their ugly heads again, or perhaps new ones will appear.

Take care of yourself and remember that a healthy lifestyle will ward off most issues and protect you from many diseases.

January

New York Time		
Calendar Day	Lunar Day	Lunar Day Start Time
01/01/24	21	10.18 PM
02/01/24	22	11.16 PM
04/01/24	23	12.14 AM
05/01/24	24	1.14 AM
06/01/24	25	2.16 AM
07/01/24	26	3.20 AM
08/01/24	27	4.26 AM
09/01/24	28	5.30 AM
10/01/24	29	6.31 AM
11/01/24	1	6.58 AM
11/01/24	2	7.26 AM
12/01/24	3	8.13 AM
13/01/24	4	8.53 AM
14/01/24	5	9.27 AM
15/01/24	6	9.59 AM
16/01/24	7	10.29 AM
17/01/24	8	10.58 AM
18/01/24	9	11.29 AM
19/01/24	10	12.04 PM
20/01/24	11	12.42 PM
21/01/24	12	1.26 PM
22/01/24	13	2.16 PM
23/01/24	14	3.11 PM
24/01/24	15	4.10 PM
25/01/24	16	5.10 PM
26/01/24	17	6.10 PM
27/01/24	18	7.10 PM
28/01/24	19	8.08 PM
29/01/24	20	9.06 PM
30/01/24	21	10.04 PM
31/01/24	22	11.02 PM

London Time		
Calendar Day	Lunar Day	Lunar Day Start Time
01/01/24	21	10.02 PM
02/01/24	22	11.08 PM
04/01/24	23	12.14 AM
05/01/24	24	1.22 AM
06/01/24	25	2.32 AM
07/01/24	26	3.44 AM
08/01/24	27	4.57 AM
09/01/24	28	6.07 AM
10/01/24	29	7.10 AM
11/01/24	30	8.03 AM
11/01/24	1	11.58 AM
12/01/24	2	8.44 AM
13/01/24	3	9.16 AM
14/01/24	4	9.42 AM
15/01/24	5	10.05 AM
16/01/24	6	10.25 AM
17/01/24	7	10.45 AM
18/01/24	8	11.07 AM
19/01/24	9	11.32 AM
20/01/24	10	12.02 PM
21/01/24	11	12.39 PM
22/01/24	12	1.25 PM
23/01/24	13	2.19 PM
24/01/24	14	3.21 PM
25/01/24	15	4.27 PM
26/01/24	16	5.35 PM
27/01/24	17	6.43 PM
28/01/24	18	7.50 PM
29/01/24	19	8.56 PM
30/01/24	20	10.01 PM
31/01/24	21	11.08 PM

You can find the description of each lunar day in the chapter "A Guide to The Moon Cycle and Lunar Days"

The stars are promising an exciting, active, and productive month for you, both at work and in your personal and romantic life.

Work

The first week of January might look somewhat uncertain, perhaps due to the traditional holiday period, when you will see some time off and get to relax.

For the rest of the month, however, you will be busy. You might go on a trip, where you will meet the people you need, or renew your relationships with previous business partners.

People with connections, influence, and money will appear on your horizon, and they might help take your business to the next level.

The astrologist also urges you to be more attentive, especially when it comes to long-term cooperation, construction, or various real estate operations. When discussing any future projects or signing important papers, be sure to carefully study each item, and consult a good lawyer if you have any doubts at all.

Expect to see things pick up if you are an employee, as well. You are climbing the ladder and there is more work to be done. A small raise might also be in order.

Money

You are seeing a lot of ups and downs in your finances this month. Your income is not the issue – that is not changing. Rather, you will be spending significantly more than usual. That may be related to various holiday activities, or possibly addressing your children's and loved ones' needs.

Love and family

Important things are happening in your personal life, as well. Those who are single and have been disappointed by previous entanglements can count on a fateful encounter, and that may happen on a trip or with people from somewhere faraway. This time, things are on a path toward marriage or something lasting and profound.

Those who are already partnered up can strengthen their relationship and a loved one will play a key role in this. Your partner is seeing positive changes at work and is more than willing to share that success with you.

Any trips planned in January will be a success, especially if you plan on going somewhere you have been before.

Your relationship with relatives will become more important. Many Scorpios will be in touch with family members living faraway and may even go visit them.

Health

In January, you are feeling energetic, adventurous, and ready to move mountains. It comes as no surprise, therefore, that you have no reason to fear falling ill.

February

New York Time			London Time		
Calendar Day	Lunar Day	Lunar Day Start Time	Calendar Day	Lunar Day	Lunar Day Start Time
02/02/24	23	12.02 AM	02/02/24	22	12.16 AM
03/02/24	24	1.04 AM	03/02/24	23	1.25 AM
04/02/24	25	2.07 AM	04/02/24	24	2.36 AM
05/02/24	26	3.11 AM	05/02/24	25	3.46 AM
06/02/24	27	4.12 AM	06/02/24	26	4.51 AM
07/02/24	28	5.10 AM	07/02/24	27	5.48 AM
08/02/24	29	6.00 AM	08/02/24	28	6.35 AM
09/02/24	30	6.44 AM	09/02/24	29	7.12 AM
09/02/24	1	6.00 PM	09/02/24	1	11.00 PM
10/02/24	2	7.22 AM	10/02/24	2	7.41 AM
11/02/24	3	7.56 AM	11/02/24	3	8.06 AM
12/02/24	4	8.28 AM	12/02/24	4	8.28 AM
13/02/24	5	8.59 AM	13/02/24	5	8.49 AM
14/02/24	6	9.30 AM	14/02/24	6	9.11 AM
15/02/24	7	10.04 AM	15/02/24	7	9.36 AM
16/02/24	8	10.42 AM	16/02/24	8	10.05 AM
17/02/24	9	11.25 AM	17/02/24	9	10.39 AM
18/02/24	10	12.13 PM	18/02/24	10	11.22 AM
19/02/24	11	1.06 PM	19/02/24	11	12.14 PM
20/02/24	12	2.03 PM	20/02/24	12	1.13 PM
21/02/24	13	3.03 PM	21/02/24	13	2.18 PM
22/02/24	14	4.03 PM	22/02/24	14	3.25 PM
23/02/24	15	5.02 PM	23/02/24	15	4.32 PM
24/02/24	16	6.01 PM	24/02/24	16	5.39 PM
25/02/24	17	6.59 PM	25/02/24	17	6.45 PM
26/02/24	18	7.57 PM	26/02/24	18	7.51 PM
27/02/24	19	8.55 PM	27/02/24	19	8.57 PM
28/02/24	20	9.54 PM	28/02/24	20	10.04 PM
29/02/24	21	10.54 PM	29/02/24	21	11.13 PM

You can find the description of each lunar day in the chapter "A Guide to The Moon Cycle and Lunar Days"

This month, your minimum responsibility is to maintain an emotional balance in the face of any situation you may face. Your inner peace is the key to stability this month, both at work and at home.

Work

Many Scorpios will be more focused on their personal life this month. Therefore, the stars recommend that you take a few days off to calmly focus on your family.

If that is not possible, the stars suggest that you tread lightly with any business partners. Conflicts are likely all month long, and it may be over a real estate dispute. It is hard to predict exactly what will happen but expect the unexpected.

Your relationships with colleagues from other cities or abroad are coming along nicely and things are looking promising.

Money

Financially, February is a neutral month for you. You will have an income, as usual, but don't expect any windfalls. Your expenses are modest, and most of them are related to your personal life.

Love and family

Your personal and family life is the focus during this cold, winter month. However, things are looking less than tranquil. Many Scorpios will be busy with home repairs, building a summer home, or dealing with other household tasks.

Spouses may have differing views on how their home should look, or perhaps regarding their family relationship in general. Arguments might be the backdrop of the entire month, though you will be able to sit down and have a calm chat. The astrologist cannot predict how things will turn out, however. Your partner is stubborn, and that can easily agitate you.

If things seem to spiral out of control, your children or perhaps an older relative might serve as a mediator. Thanks to their efforts, things might have quieted down by March.

Unmarried couples might run into arguments with their parents, who might be less than thrilled with the way things stand. By March, you will be done with this obstacle course, and it should be smooth sailing.

This applies to all problems this month, whether work-related or within your family.

Health

In February, you will not be feeling particularly energetic, but you are also not vulnerable to any serious illnesses, so long as you make sure to get enough sleep or let yourself be overcome with emotions.

The best investment you can make this month is a vacation, perhaps a plane ticket somewhere warm, or even the neighboring town. Spend a few days away from work and come back feeling fresh and renewed.

March

New York Time				London Time		
Calendar Day	Lunar Day	Lunar Day Start Time		Calendar Day	Lunar Day	Lunar Day Start Time
01/03/24	22	11.56 PM		02/03/24	22	12.22 AM
03/03/24	23	12.57 AM		03/03/24	23	1.30 AM
04/03/24	24	1.58 AM		04/03/24	24	2.36 AM
05/03/24	25	2.55 AM		05/03/24	25	3.35 AM
06/03/24	26	3.48 AM		06/03/24	26	4.25 AM
07/03/24	27	4.34 AM		07/03/24	27	5.05 AM
08/03/24	28	5.14 AM		08/03/24	28	5.38 AM
09/03/24	29	5.50 AM		09/03/24	29	6.05 AM
10/03/24	1	4.02 AM		10/03/24	30	6.28 AM
10/03/24	2	6.23 AM		10/03/24	1	9.02 AM
11/03/24	3	6.55 AM		11/03/24	2	6.50 AM
12/03/24	4	7.27 AM		12/03/24	3	7.12 AM
13/03/24	5	8.01 AM		13/03/24	4	7.36 AM
14/03/24	6	8.38 AM		14/03/24	5	8.04 AM
15/03/24	7	9.21 AM		15/03/24	6	8.37 AM
16/03/24	8	10.08 AM		16/03/24	7	9.19 AM
17/03/24	9	11.01 AM		17/03/24	8	10.08 AM
18/03/24	10	11.57 AM		18/03/24	9	11.06 AM
19/03/24	11	12.56 PM		19/03/24	10	12.09 PM
20/03/24	12	1.56 PM		20/03/24	11	1.16 PM
21/03/24	13	2.55 PM		21/03/24	12	2.23 PM
22/03/24	14	3.54 PM		22/03/24	13	3.30 PM
23/03/24	15	4.52 PM		23/03/24	14	4.36 PM
24/03/24	16	5.50 PM		24/03/24	15	5.42 PM
25/03/24	17	6.48 PM		25/03/24	16	6.48 PM
26/03/24	18	7.47 PM		26/03/24	17	7.55 PM
27/03/24	19	8.47 PM		27/03/24	18	9.03 PM
28/03/24	20	9.48 PM		28/03/24	19	10.12 PM
29/03/24	21	10.50 PM		29/03/24	20	11.21 PM
30/03/24	22	11.50 PM		31/03/24	21	12.27 AM

You can find the description of each lunar day in the chapter "A Guide to The Moon Cycle and Lunar Days"

For you, March is a time to seek both inner and outer harmony. Of course, this is a tall order, but for you, nothing is impossible!

Work

The tidal wave of events this month will take you by storm. Despite your jam-packed schedule, however, you will somehow manage to keep up with it all. You are bound with energy, and attention from people whose opinions matter to you will significantly improve things for you, including your self-esteem.

The first 20 days of the month are a good time to develop old connections and meet new people, but the last 10 days will have you putting your nose to the grindstone as you resolve the most difficult tasks that will require even more diligence and knowledge.

March is a promising time for those who work in creative fields – actors, artists, journalists, and musicians. Your popularity will grow, as will your income.

Moreover, March is also a good time for those in other professions. You will be coming up with creative ideas, thinking outside the box, and showing your achievements to colleagues and a wider audience in general.

The right people will appreciate and support your creative solutions.

Money

Financially, March is not particularly noteworthy. Your income is stable, your expenses are low, and all of them are personal or pleasant in nature. You will be spending money on relaxation, your children, and your loved one – that will require some money, but there's no way around it. And the best way to spend your money is on your loved ones, and, naturally, yourself.

Love and family

Many Scorpios will be more focused on their home and family or romantic relationships this month.

Those who are immersed in day-to-day matters might occasionally have as spat, but in the end, you will find a compromise. Your children will require your attention and some action on your part to resolve their problems, and this concerns even couples on the rocks.

Your relationship with your romantic partner will settle down, and many couples will start taking steps toward marriage.

Friction with your parents is highly likely from March 9 to 12, but things should be smoothed over by the end of the month.

Most Scorpios will see a lot of changes in their social circles. The stars recommend that you attend more parties than usual and take care to always look your best. You are in the limelight and making a great impression on everyone worth talking to!

Those who don't have a steady partner can count on luck this month. Those who aren't single may find themselves tempted. The choice is yours.

Be sensitive to your loved ones, and you will be pleased with their response.

Health

You are feeling energetic in March and have no reason to fear falling ill. You might feel a bit tired from all of the hustle and bustle during the last 10 days of the month, and especially during the Full Moon and eclipse from March 24-26. During this time, take care of yourself and practice moderation.

April

New York Time			London Time		
Calendar Day	Lunar Day	Lunar Day Start Time	Calendar Day	Lunar Day	Lunar Day Start Time
01/04/24	23	12.48 AM	01/04/24	22	2.27 AM
02/04/24	24	1.40 AM	02/04/24	23	3.19 AM
03/04/24	25	2.27 AM	03/04/24	24	4.02 AM
04/04/24	26	3.08 AM	04/04/24	25	4.36 AM
05/04/24	27	3.44 AM	05/04/24	26	5.04 AM
06/04/24	28	4.18 AM	06/04/24	27	5.28 AM
07/04/24	29	4.49 AM	07/04/24	28	5.50 AM
08/04/24	30	5.21 AM	08/04/24	29	6.12 AM
08/04/24	1	2.23 PM	08/04/24	1	7.23 PM
09/04/24	2	6.54 AM	09/04/24	2	6.35 AM
10/04/24	3	7.31 AM	10/04/24	3	7.01 AM
11/04/24	4	8.12 AM	11/04/24	4	7.32 AM
12/04/24	5	8.58 AM	12/04/24	5	8.11 AM
13/04/24	6	9.50 AM	13/04/24	6	8.58 AM
14/04/24	7	10.47 AM	14/04/24	7	9.55 AM
15/04/24	8	11.47 AM	15/04/24	8	10.58 AM
16/04/24	9	12.47 PM	16/04/24	9	12.04 PM
17/04/24	10	1.47 PM	17/04/24	10	1.12 PM
18/04/24	11	2.46 PM	18/04/24	11	2.19 PM
19/04/24	12	3.45 PM	19/04/24	12	3.26 PM
20/04/24	13	4.43 PM	20/04/24	13	4.32 PM
21/04/24	14	5.41 PM	21/04/24	14	5.38 PM
22/04/24	15	6.40 PM	22/04/24	15	6.45 PM
23/04/24	16	7.40 PM	23/04/24	16	7.53 PM
24/04/24	17	8.41 PM	24/04/24	17	9.02 PM
25/04/24	18	9.43 PM	25/04/24	18	10.12 PM
26/04/24	19	10.45 PM	26/04/24	19	11.20 PM
27/04/24	20	11.43 PM	28/04/24	20	12.22 AM
29/04/24	21	12.37 AM	29/04/24	21	1.17 AM
30/04/24	22	1.25 AM	30/04/24	22	2.02 AM

You can find the description of each lunar day in the chapter "A Guide to The Moon Cycle and Lunar Days"

Remember this month that slow and steady wins the race. Haste makes waste. This month, you might experience some losses and need extra time even for simple tasks.

Work

April is a time for burdensome, fastidious tasks, when you have to put out various fires that fate sends your way. You might have to come back to the same issues time and again or make corrections on work you already started. The stars predict that it will all turn out brilliantly, and in time, those around you will understand. Right now, however, is the time to focus on the details and don't let anything slip through the cracks.

Managers would be wise to keep an eye on subordinates, and, if you can, keep your finger on the pulse of things.

Employees will work in a team, and be sure to carefully follow the instructions, especially when it comes to red tape and financial documents.

In late April, you will see new business partners on your horizon, or perhaps someone from the past. The stars recommend you remain vigilant for any invitations they offer, which may be financially very attractive.

Money

Financially, April is neutral. You have a stable and predictable income, and your expenses are modest, and mostly related to your personal life.

Expect the largest sums on April 1, 8, 9, 16-18, 26, and 27.

Love and family

The eclipse this month will take place in the sector of the sky responsible for work and tiresome everyday tasks. During the first half of the month, you may not have time for much of a personal life.

During the second half, however, those with families will be immersed in their children's affairs, and they may have to help adult children or care for younger family members.

Your relationship with family members is stable, without any major ups or downs.

Single people might meet someone new, and the last 10 days of April and all of May is when this is most likely to happen. In addition to new encounters, you might also run into someone from your past, and your relationship may be much more interesting and improved this time around.

Health

In April, you are feeling sluggish, especially if you are elderly or weakened. You should be more careful during the New Moon and eclipse from April 7-9. Those who are young and healthy should lead a healthy lifestyle and take good care of themselves.

May

New York Time			London Time		
Calendar Day	Lunar Day	Lunar Day Start Time	Calendar Day	Lunar Day	Lunar Day Start Time
01/05/24	23	2.07 AM	01/05/24	23	2.38 AM
02/05/24	24	2.43 AM	02/05/24	24	3.07 AM
03/05/24	25	3.16 AM	03/05/24	25	3.31 AM
04/05/24	26	3.47 AM	04/05/24	26	3.53 AM
05/05/24	27	4.18 AM	05/05/24	27	4.14 AM
06/05/24	28	4.49 AM	06/05/24	28	4.35 AM
07/05/24	29	5.23 AM	07/05/24	29	4.59 AM
07/05/24	1	11.24 PM	08/05/24	1	4.24 AM
08/05/24	2	6.02 AM	08/05/24	2	5.27 AM
09/05/24	3	6.46 AM	09/05/24	3	6.02 AM
10/05/24	4	7.36 AM	10/05/24	4	6.46 AM
11/05/24	5	8.33 AM	11/05/24	5	7.39 AM
12/05/24	6	9.33 AM	12/05/24	6	8.41 AM
13/05/24	7	10.34 AM	13/05/24	7	9.48 AM
14/05/24	8	11.36 AM	14/05/24	8	10.57 AM
15/05/24	9	12.36 PM	15/05/24	9	12.06 PM
16/05/24	10	1.35 PM	16/05/24	10	1.13 PM
17/05/24	11	2.33 PM	17/05/24	11	2.19 PM
18/05/24	12	3.31 PM	18/05/24	12	3.25 PM
19/05/24	13	4.29 PM	19/05/24	13	4.32 PM
20/05/24	14	5.29 PM	20/05/24	14	5.39 PM
21/05/24	15	6.31 PM	21/05/24	15	6.49 PM
22/05/24	16	7.33 PM	22/05/24	16	7.59 PM
23/05/24	17	8.36 PM	23/05/24	17	9.09 PM
24/05/24	18	9.37 PM	24/05/24	18	10.15 PM
25/05/24	19	10.33 PM	25/05/24	19	11.13 PM
26/05/24	20	11.24 PM	27/05/24	20	12.02 AM
28/05/24	21	12.07 AM	28/05/24	21	12.40 AM
29/05/24	22	12.45 AM	29/05/24	22	1.11 AM
30/05/24	23	1.19 AM	30/05/24	23	1.36 AM
31/05/24	24	1.50 AM	31/05/24	24	1.58 AM

You can find the description of each lunar day in the chapter "A Guide to The Moon Cycle and Lunar Days"

May is an unusual month for you. You are seeing major changes at home, at work, and in your surroundings. As they say, it's all for the best.

Work

The most important thing this month is your relationship with business partners. The ability to listen, understand, and even give in a little from time to time is the key to success, both now and in the future. You might be surrounded by all different kinds of people – both new acquaintances and partners from the past.

Business owners and managers will be planning on expanding their business, and that will likely entail major purchases and various real estate transactions. This month, you may count on both moral and financial support from business partners.

Employees may be thinking about a new job, but things will not happen so quickly. More likely, you might be thinking about taking some time away from your current job, either due to family business or simply a long leave of absence.

Alternatively, you might find work under the wing of an old friend, where things are also undergoing changes.

Money

May is looking very turbulent for your wallet. You won't end up bankrupt, but you will be spending a lot due to business partners, parents, or perhaps a loved one.

You might have some profits from successful real estate transactions, or perhaps receive some very favorable terms of credit or an inheritance.

Love and family

Your personal life may be more important to you than work in May. Those with families will be addressing issues related to your home and taking steps in that direction. A loved one may play a major role here, and you would be wise to follow his or her lead.

Some Scorpios will be thinking about a new addition to the family, and this year, those plans will come to life.

Those who are single or have been let down by love in the past are in for an exciting and unusual time.

You are very likely to have a fateful encounter in May, and there is a chance that it will lead to deep feelings and even marriage.

Your relationship with an old flame is not entirely over, but in the next three to four months, it will gradually fade away.

Your relationship with older children is noticeably improved, and you might see each other frequently and make your peace, if you recently had an argument or went your separate ways.

Health

This month, you have no reason to fear for your health, but in the last 10 days of the month, you might feel tired from all of the hustle and bustle.

If that is your case, spend a few days away focused on yourself.

June

New York Time			London Time		
Calendar Day	Lunar Day	Lunar Day Start Time	Calendar Day	Lunar Day	Lunar Day Start Time
01/06/24	25	2.19 AM	01/06/24	25	2.19 AM
02/06/24	26	2.49 AM	02/06/24	26	2.39 AM
03/06/24	27	3.21 AM	03/06/24	27	3.01 AM
04/06/24	28	3.56 AM	04/06/24	28	3.26 AM
05/06/24	29	4.37 AM	05/06/24	29	3.57 AM
06/06/24	30	5.24 AM	06/06/24	30	4.36 AM
06/06/24	1	8.40 AM	06/06/24	1	1.40 PM
07/06/24	2	6.18 AM	07/06/24	2	5.25 AM
08/06/24	3	7.17 AM	08/06/24	3	6.24 AM
09/06/24	4	8.19 AM	09/06/24	4	7.30 AM
10/06/24	5	9.22 AM	10/06/24	5	8.39 AM
11/06/24	6	10.23 AM	11/06/24	6	9.49 AM
12/06/24	7	11.23 AM	12/06/24	7	10.58 AM
13/06/24	8	12.22 PM	13/06/24	8	12.05 PM
14/06/24	9	1.20 PM	14/06/24	9	1.11 PM
15/06/24	10	2.18 PM	15/06/24	10	2.17 PM
16/06/24	11	3.17 PM	16/06/24	11	3.24 PM
17/06/24	12	4.17 PM	17/06/24	12	4.32 PM
18/06/24	13	5.19 PM	18/06/24	13	5.42 PM
19/06/24	14	6.22 PM	19/06/24	14	6.53 PM
20/06/24	15	7.25 PM	20/06/24	15	8.01 PM
21/06/24	16	8.24 PM	21/06/24	16	9.04 PM
22/06/24	17	9.18 PM	22/06/24	17	9.57 PM
23/06/24	18	10.06 PM	23/06/24	18	10.40 PM
24/06/24	19	10.46 PM	24/06/24	19	11.14 PM
25/06/24	20	11.22 PM	25/06/24	20	11.42 PM
26/06/24	21	11.53 PM	27/06/24	21	12.05 AM
28/06/24	22	12.23 AM	28/06/24	22	12.25 AM
29/06/24	23	12.52 AM	29/06/24	23	12.45 AM
30/06/24	24	1.23 AM	30/06/24	24	1.06 AM

You can find the description of each lunar day in the chapter "A Guide to The Moon Cycle and Lunar Days"

You are embarking on one of the most difficult months of the year, so it is best not to rush things. The key to stability both at work and in your relationships is to strike an inner balance.

Work

The stars' influence will be most felt when it comes to relaxation and your personal affairs this month.

But if you have to work anyway, the best thing you can do in June is focus on administrative tasks, get your office in order, or spruce up other production spaces.

Business owners and managers will be thinking about expanding their business and taking the first steps in that direction. You will be busy with various real estate transactions or acquiring the best land, which will help grow your business more successfully.

Employees might be thinking about leaving their job to work for a quieter company, perhaps a family business, and opportunities will arise during the last 10 days of the month. From June 20-30 is the best time to start talking to your contacts in other cities or abroad, and you might take a successful trip.

Money

Financially, the second 10 days of June will be a mess for you. During this time, many Scorpios will lose a large sum of money, and most likely, that will be due to your personal life, family demands, or most likely, your children.

Nonetheless, you will not end up in the red, and during the first 10 days, you might actually come into a decent profit from a real estate transaction. You can expect support from your parents, a loved one, or favorable terms of credit, as well.

Love and family

Most Scorpios will be much more focused on home and family this month. You might be busy with repairs, changing up the interior, or even drawing up plans related to a move.

Stormy skies loom ahead during the second 10 days of June. From the 8th to 11, you might unexpectedly experience arguments, which will have longstanding consequences.

The stars recommend that couples, whether they are married or not, tread lightly and avoid pushing your loved one's buttons.

During this time, you may experience trouble involving your children, and that will involve spending a large amount of money. This situation does not look like it will be short-lived, so be attentive to your younger children, and help your older ones however they need it.

Health

In June, you are feeling sluggish, and the most difficult time will be in the middle of the month. During this time, take care of yourself and take any precaution you can.

During the last 10 days of the month, things will be much more favorable. Your energy will be back, and the exhaustion will fade away.

July

New York Time

Calendar Day	Lunar Day	Lunar Day Start Time
01/07/24	25	1.56 AM
02/07/24	26	2.34 AM
03/07/24	27	3.17 AM
04/07/24	28	4.07 AM
05/07/24	29	5.03 AM
05/07/24	1	6.59 PM
06/07/24	2	6.04 AM
07/07/24	3	7.07 AM
08/07/24	4	8.10 AM
09/07/24	5	9.11 AM
10/07/24	6	10.11 AM
11/07/24	7	11.09 AM
12/07/24	8	12.07 PM
13/07/24	9	1.05 PM
14/07/24	10	2.04 PM
15/07/24	11	3.04 PM
16/07/24	12	4.06 PM
17/07/24	13	5.09 PM
18/07/24	14	6.10 PM
19/07/24	15	7.07 PM
20/07/24	16	7.58 PM
21/07/24	17	8.42 PM
22/07/24	18	9.21 PM
23/07/24	19	9.55 PM
24/07/24	20	10.26 PM
25/07/24	21	10.56 PM
26/07/24	22	11.26 PM
27/07/24	23	11.58 PM
29/07/24	24	12.34 AM
30/07/24	25	1.15 AM
31/07/24	26	2.03 AM

London Time

Calendar Day	Lunar Day	Lunar Day Start Time
01/07/24	25	1.30 AM
02/07/24	26	1.58 AM
03/07/24	27	2.32 AM
04/07/24	28	3.16 AM
05/07/24	29	4.10 AM
05/07/24	1	11.59 PM
06/07/24	2	5.13 AM
07/07/24	3	6.21 AM
08/07/24	4	7.32 AM
09/07/24	5	8.42 AM
10/07/24	6	9.50 AM
11/07/24	7	10.57 AM
12/07/24	8	12.03 PM
13/07/24	9	1.09 PM
14/07/24	10	2.16 PM
15/07/24	11	3.24 PM
16/07/24	12	4.34 PM
17/07/24	13	5.43 PM
18/07/24	14	6.48 PM
19/07/24	15	7.46 PM
20/07/24	16	8.35 PM
21/07/24	17	9.13 PM
22/07/24	18	9.44 PM
23/07/24	19	10.09 PM
24/07/24	20	10.31 PM
25/07/24	21	10.52 PM
26/07/24	22	11.12 PM
27/07/24	23	11.35 PM
29/07/24	24	12.01 AM
30/07/24	25	12.33 AM
31/07/24	26	1.14 AM

You can find the description of each lunar day in the chapter "A Guide to The Moon Cycle and Lunar Days"

This month, you are overcome with a desire for movement and change. That's no surprise – sitting still and doing the same thing over and over again is not your style!

Work

Despite all of the administrative tasks that you still have to deal with, you are now busy with traveling and active communication with colleagues from other cities and abroad. The great news is that right now, you can be sure to receive support from leaders and power structures, and other powers that be. Your ability to negotiate and get along with others is especially important right now. All of that means that July is a time of great success and promise.

There's another plus here – July is a great time for reconnecting with old friends and making new acquaintances.

It is possible that all of this will happen on a trip or among people from somewhere far away.

If you want a new job or new responsibilities, you will be busy with negotiations and laying the groundwork to make a move later on.

Money

Financially, July is a neutral month. Your income is modest, though your expenses are also low. The astrologist predicts that in some cases, you will be investing in business, or possibly your personal life.

Love and family

July is a great time for your personal life, too. Your relationship with your partner or spouse is much better these days, and you might even describe things as idyllic.

Your relationship with your children is also much better. If you recently had a serious argument, now might be the time to reconcile.

Children and parents who have been separated by time and distance will have a happy reunion. You might take a trip, which will be a great success.

If you want to and are able to take time off to relax, the best destination is somewhere you have been before, in order to avoid being disappointed or other problems.

Health

This month, you are feeling significantly better, and any illnesses from last month will be an unhappy memory.

August

New York Time				London Time		
Calendar Day	Lunar Day	Lunar Day Start Time		Calendar Day	Lunar Day	Lunar Day Start Time
01/08/24	27	2.56 AM		01/08/24	27	2.03 AM
02/08/24	28	3.54 AM		02/08/24	28	3.02 AM
03/08/24	29	4.56 AM		03/08/24	29	4.08 AM
04/08/24	30	5.58 AM		04/08/24	30	5.17 AM
04/08/24	1	7.14 AM		04/08/24	1	12.14 PM
05/08/24	2	7.00 AM		05/08/24	2	6.27 AM
06/08/24	3	8.00 AM		06/08/24	3	7.36 AM
07/08/24	4	8.59 AM		07/08/24	4	8.43 AM
08/08/24	5	9.57 AM		08/08/24	5	9.50 AM
09/08/24	6	10.55 AM		09/08/24	6	10.55 AM
10/08/24	7	11.53 AM		10/08/24	7	12.02 PM
11/08/24	8	12.52 PM		11/08/24	8	1.09 PM
12/08/24	9	1.52 PM		12/08/24	9	2.17 PM
13/08/24	10	2.54 PM		13/08/24	10	3.25 PM
14/08/24	11	3.54 PM		14/08/24	11	4.31 PM
15/08/24	12	4.52 PM		15/08/24	12	5.32 PM
16/08/24	13	5.46 PM		16/08/24	13	6.24 PM
17/08/24	14	6.33 PM		17/08/24	14	7.07 PM
18/08/24	15	7.15 PM		18/08/24	15	7.42 PM
19/08/24	16	7.51 PM		19/08/24	16	8.10 PM
20/08/24	17	8.24 PM		20/08/24	17	8.33 PM
21/08/24	18	8.56 PM		21/08/24	18	8.55 PM
22/08/24	19	9.27 PM		22/08/24	19	9.17 PM
23/08/24	20	9.59 PM		23/08/24	20	9.39 PM
24/08/24	21	10.35 PM		24/08/24	21	10.05 PM
25/08/24	22	11.15 PM		25/08/24	22	10.35 PM
27/08/24	23	12.00 AM		26/08/24	23	11.13 PM
28/08/24	24	12.52 AM		28/08/24	24	12.00 AM
29/08/24	25	1.48 AM		29/08/24	25	12.56 AM
30/08/24	26	2.48 AM		30/08/24	26	1.59 AM
31/08/24	27	3.50 AM		31/08/24	27	3.07 AM

You can find the description of each lunar day in the chapter "A Guide to The Moon Cycle and Lunar Days"

August will have you facing off with a series of unrelated tasks. So keep yourself in check, concentrate, and keep everything under control. After all, you can do it!

Work

You are busy at work, but things aren't easy.

Business owners and leaders will have to resolve difficult financial issues, as well as challenging relationships that may have developed among close friends.

You might also face setbacks at work, difficulties with auditing agencies, or someone highly placed in society. Alternatively, you may not have the people you need when you need them.

Employees will be seeing changes at work, and perhaps there will be changes to management or the direction your employer is headed. During this time, the stars recommend that you work meticulously on your own duties and keep an eye on any important paperwork.

Mercury will be in retrograde for most of August, which heightens the risk of mistakes, misunderstandings with your contacts, and that can be reflected both at work and in your relationship with many people.

Money

August will be ruinous. You will be bleeding money in every direction, while earning less.

However, you can count on receiving something on August 4, 5, 13-15, and 29-31.

Love and family

Scorpios who are focused on their personal life are also in store for unpleasant surprises. Parents will face trouble with their children, and this will involve a lot of expense, too.

Perhaps, your child will be going through a tough time, and you will have to support him or her, both morally and financially.

Alternatively, you might find yourself having blowouts with your partner.

Couples will face a series of stressors, which will reach a crescendo during the second half of the month.

Most Scorpios should remember that by mid-August, your anxiety will be on the rise, and you will need to keep yourself in check, which will not be easy. If you want to hold onto your relationships, do not react. The stars recommend that you keep a cool head and act diplomatically.

If you have been on the rocks with your partner for some time, however, and you have no desire to continue with him or her, then just let things play out.

Health

This month, your main problem will be your emotions and turbulence, which will literally permeate the atmosphere. That might leave even the strongest Scorpios feeling shaken, so spend more time in nature and remember wise King Solomon, who said that to everything, there is a season.

September

New York Time			London Time		
Calendar Day	Lunar Day	Lunar Day Start Time	Calendar Day	Lunar Day	Lunar Day Start Time
01/09/24	28	4.51 AM	01/09/24	28	4.16 AM
02/09/24	29	5.52 AM	02/09/24	29	5.25 AM
02/09/24	1	9.56 PM	03/09/24	1	2.56 AM
03/09/24	2	6.51 AM	03/09/24	2	6.32 AM
04/09/24	3	7.49 AM	04/09/24	3	7.39 AM
05/09/24	4	8.47 AM	05/09/24	4	8.45 AM
06/09/24	5	9.45 AM	06/09/24	5	9.51 AM
07/09/24	6	10.43 AM	07/09/24	6	10.57 AM
08/09/24	7	11.43 AM	08/09/24	7	12.04 PM
09/09/24	8	12.42 PM	09/09/24	8	1.11 PM
10/09/24	9	1.42 PM	10/09/24	9	2.17 PM
11/09/24	10	2.40 PM	11/09/24	10	3.19 PM
12/09/24	11	3.34 PM	12/09/24	11	4.14 PM
13/09/24	12	4.23 PM	13/09/24	12	5.00 PM
14/09/24	13	5.06 PM	14/09/24	13	5.37 PM
15/09/24	14	5.44 PM	15/09/24	14	6.07 PM
16/09/24	15	6.19 PM	16/09/24	15	6.33 PM
17/09/24	16	6.51 PM	17/09/24	16	6.56 PM
18/09/24	17	7.23 PM	18/09/24	17	7.18 PM
19/09/24	18	7.56 PM	19/09/24	18	7.40 PM
20/09/24	19	8.31 PM	20/09/24	19	8.05 PM
21/09/24	20	9.11 PM	21/09/24	20	8.35 PM
22/09/24	21	9.56 PM	22/09/24	21	9.11 PM
23/09/24	22	10.46 PM	23/09/24	22	9.55 PM
24/09/24	23	11.42 PM	24/09/24	23	10.49 PM
26/09/24	24	12.42 AM	25/09/24	24	11.51 PM
27/09/24	25	1.44 AM	27/09/24	25	12.58 AM
28/09/24	26	2.45 AM	28/09/24	26	2.07 AM
29/09/24	27	3.45 AM	29/09/24	27	3.16 AM
30/09/24	28	4.44 AM	30/09/24	28	4.23 AM

You can find the description of each lunar day in the chapter "A Guide to The Moon Cycle and Lunar Days"

During the first month of Autumn, things are not exactly going your way, and your problems from August will have to be resolved, one way or another. The pendulum will not swing in the other direction until late September, so hold your defenses, if you are unable to go on the offense just yet.

Work

For most Scorpios, your main task at work is still financial in nature. You might face demands from business partners, friends, or someone highly placed in society. Most of this is likely to be clearly material in nature, and you will have to reckon with it one way or another.

Employees should refrain from any criticism of their managers or arguing with colleagues. You might not be entirely objective, but even if you are in the right, it is worth defending your position diplomatically and avoiding any conflict or quarrels. That recommendation goes for all Scorpios, regardless of your field.

Your relationship with colleagues in other cities or abroad is coming along well, and in mid-September, you might take a trip, where you will hold a series of favorable and very necessary meetings.

Money

September is a ruinous month for your pocketbook. You might be bleeding money in every direction, and lots of it. You may need to settle old debts and shoulder your material obligations, or alternatively, you will be putting up the lion's share of the resources for your business development.

Those who are not part of the working world will spend money on their children and loved ones.

Love and family

During this quiet month, many Scorpios will be more focused on their personal life.

Parents will continue to deal with problems involving their children, who will require large amounts of spending. It is impossible to predict what will happen in each individual case, but there is reason for concern here.

Be attentive to the younger members of your family and be sure to provide extra support for the elder ones, who may be going through some difficulties right now. Gloomy Saturn, which is spending a long time in the sector of the sky responsible for the new generation, is to blame.

Couples might find themselves constantly arguing, and one of these spats may be your last. The eclipse and Full Moon will bring tension to all relationships from September 16-18, and these are days full of excessive emotions, when any slip of the tongue may provoke an all-out conflict. Remember this and think 100 times before you open your mouth or make a move. Scorpio is an emotional sign, and all of its representatives would be wise to heed this advice.

During the last part of the month, or perhaps early in October, you might take a trip or meet with loved ones who live in another city or abroad.

Health

This month, you are not feeling particularly energetic, but if you live a healthy lifestyle, you will not face any complications.

October

New York Time			London Time		
Calendar Day	Lunar Day	Lunar Day Start Time	Calendar Day	Lunar Day	Lunar Day Start Time
01/10/24	29	5.42 AM	01/10/24	29	5.30 AM
02/10/24	30	6.40 AM	02/10/24	30	6.35 AM
02/10/24	1	1.50 PM	02/10/24	1	7.50 PM
03/10/24	2	6.38 AM	03/10/24	2	7.41 AM
04/10/24	3	7.36 AM	04/10/24	3	8.48 AM
05/10/24	4	8.36 AM	05/10/24	4	9.55 AM
06/10/24	5	9.35 AM	06/10/24	5	11.02 AM
07/10/24	6	10.35 AM	07/10/24	6	12.08 PM
08/10/24	7	11.32 AM	08/10/24	7	1.11 PM
09/10/24	8	12.26 PM	09/10/24	8	2.07 PM
10/10/24	9	1.16 PM	10/10/24	9	2.55 PM
11/10/24	10	2.00 PM	11/10/24	10	3.34 PM
12/10/24	11	2.39 PM	12/10/24	11	4.06 PM
13/10/24	12	3.14 PM	13/10/24	12	4.33 PM
14/10/24	13	3.46 PM	14/10/24	13	4.56 PM
15/10/24	14	4.18 PM	15/10/24	14	5.18 PM
16/10/24	15	4.50 PM	16/10/24	15	5.40 PM
17/10/24	16	5.24 PM	17/10/24	16	6.03 PM
18/10/24	17	6.02 PM	18/10/24	17	6.31 PM
19/10/24	18	6.46 PM	19/10/24	18	7.04 PM
20/10/24	19	7.36 PM	20/10/24	19	7.46 PM
21/10/24	20	8.32 PM	21/10/24	20	8.38 PM
22/10/24	21	9.32 PM	22/10/24	21	9.39 PM
23/10/24	22	10.34 PM	23/10/24	22	10.47 PM
24/10/24	23	11.37 PM	24/10/24	23	11.56 PM
26/10/24	24	12.38 AM	26/10/24	24	1.06 AM
27/10/24	25	1.38 AM	27/10/24	25	1.14 AM
28/10/24	26	2.36 AM	28/10/24	26	2.20 AM
29/10/24	27	3.34 AM	29/10/24	27	3.26 AM
30/10/24	28	4.31 AM	30/10/24	28	4.32 AM
31/10/24	29	5.30 AM	31/10/24	29	5.38 AM

You can find the description of each lunar day in the chapter "A Guide to The Moon Cycle and Lunar Days"

October promises to be a quiet month filled with administrative tasks, and an opportunity to shore up your position and find your footing, both at work and in your personal life.

Work

In October, you will be able to immerse yourself in getting your affairs in order at work. Business owners and managers may find themselves climbing mountains, especially if you are currently expanding your business or busy with construction and repairs. After a busy August and September, the heavens are giving you a chance to do everything you need to do.

Your relationship with colleagues in other cities or abroad is moving along in your favor, and you might get back into touch with old acquaintances or build new ties as well. Any trips planned for October will be an enormous success.

Employees will spend most of October focused on family issues, where you will also be fairly busy. You might have to take some days off and spend time on household matters. If you have to remain at the office, lay low and avoid getting on management's nerves.

Money

October is stable when it comes to your finances, but no more. You won't come into any windfalls, but you will also not find yourself broke. Your expenses are significantly less than before, which is a positive trend set to continue into the future. You might see healthy profits from real estate transactions or favorable terms of credit.

Those who are not part of the working world can count on support from their loved ones.

Love and family

The stars predict that many Scorpios will spend most of this month focused on their personal lives and various family events.

You will be setting up a home or conducting various real estate transactions. You can expect any of these tasks to run smoothly, without any trouble or setbacks.

A tricky situation involving your children recently arose, and here, your woes seem to be easing and you are able to make a lot of progress. Most likely, things look less urgent than before. You might see your children who live in other cities or abroad.

The friendly contact between Mars and Venus will significantly improve your relationship with your partner. If you have any desire to rekindle a relationship that has cooled off, that will not be a difficult endeavor, though you will have to make the first step. If you are clear that you are willing to meet your partner, you will be pleased with his or her response.

Health

This month, you are not particularly energetic, but you have staunch support from Venus, which means that you are probably spared any serious illnesses. In any case, during the New Moon and eclipse from October 2-4, lay low and take care of yourself.

November

New York Time			London Time		
Calendar Day	Lunar Day	Lunar Day Start Time	Calendar Day	Lunar Day	Lunar Day Start Time
01/11/24	30	6.29 AM	01/11/24	30	6.45 AM
01/11/24	1	7.48 AM	01/11/24	1	12.48 PM
02/11/24	2	7.29 AM	02/11/24	2	7.53 AM
03/11/24	3	8.29 AM	03/11/24	3	9.00 AM
04/11/24	4	9.27 AM	04/11/24	4	10.04 AM
05/11/24	5	10.23 AM	05/11/24	5	11.03 AM
06/11/24	6	11.13 AM	06/11/24	6	11.53 AM
07/11/24	7	11.58 AM	07/11/24	7	12.34 PM
08/11/24	8	12.37 PM	08/11/24	8	1.08 PM
09/11/24	9	1.13 PM	09/11/24	9	1.35 PM
10/11/24	10	1.44 PM	10/11/24	10	1.58 PM
11/11/24	11	2.15 PM	11/11/24	11	2.20 PM
12/11/24	12	2.45 PM	12/11/24	12	2.40 PM
13/11/24	13	3.17 PM	13/11/24	13	3.02 PM
14/11/24	14	3.53 PM	14/11/24	14	3.27 PM
15/11/24	15	4.33 PM	15/11/24	15	3.57 PM
16/11/24	16	5.20 PM	16/11/24	16	4.35 PM
17/11/24	17	6.15 PM	17/11/24	17	5.22 PM
18/11/24	18	7.15 PM	18/11/24	18	6.21 PM
19/11/24	19	8.19 PM	19/11/24	19	7.28 PM
20/11/24	20	9.23 PM	20/11/24	20	8.39 PM
21/11/24	21	10.27 PM	21/11/24	21	9.51 PM
22/11/24	22	11.28 PM	22/11/24	22	11.01 PM
24/11/24	23	12.27 AM	24/11/24	23	12.09 AM
25/11/24	24	1.25 AM	25/11/24	24	1.15 AM
26/11/24	25	2.23 AM	26/11/24	25	2.21 AM
27/11/24	26	3.21 AM	27/11/24	26	3.27 AM
28/11/24	27	4.20 AM	28/11/24	27	4.33 AM
29/11/24	28	5.20 AM	29/11/24	28	5.41 AM
30/11/24	29	6.21 AM	30/11/24	29	6.49 AM

You can find the description of each lunar day in the chapter "A Guide to The Moon Cycle and Lunar Days"

It's common to celebrate your birth month as you ward off problems from all sides – at home, at work, and in your inner circle. But God only gives us what we can handle, so you will manage!

Work

Your main task this month will be resolving financial trouble. Business owners and managers will have to find a lot of resources in order to expand their business, but this process will continue in your favor. You might need to carry out the challenging task of reorganizing your business, which will occupy you for the near future.

Employees will see changes underway at work and be able to leverage them. This may become clear a bit later, but there are definitely opportunities on the horizon.

Your relationship with colleagues in other cities or abroad is developing the way it should, and that will be noticeable in mid-November. You might take a trip or start preparing for one.

Money

You are in for some financial turbulence this month. Everyone will need money – your loved ones, children, your house!

You will spend a lot expanding your business, especially if you are a business owner.

You will still have income, but it will be barely enough to cover your expenses, and close to the end of the month, your wallet will be looking mighty thin.

Love and family

Your personal life is unstable right now, as well. Once again, parents will have to deal with trouble involving their children, and once again, you will have to spend a lot of money to resolve it all. You will do everything in order to fix this and be largely successful.

You might see your children who live in another city or abroad.

Spouses will once again be busy with household tasks, and perhaps even work on building a new home.

This might seem like a Sisyphean task right now, but the stars predict that within six months, many of these quandaries will be resolved, and favorably! In the meantime, you are working in this direction and have more than enough resources to get it done. Remember, it costs money to save money.

Couples will experience some stormy seas. You will do everything you can for your partner to get over his or her anger, and you will have some success here. Things will continue to be unstable here for a long time to come, so you will need some patience.

Any travel with your partner in November will go well and might improve things, whether you are married or not.

Health

This month, you are feeling noticeably more energetic and any illnesses from October will fade away.

December

New York Time		
Calendar Day	Lunar Day	Lunar Day Start Time
1	01/12/24	1.22 AM
2	01/12/24	7.21 AM
3	02/12/24	8.18 AM
4	03/12/24	9.11 AM
5	04/12/24	9.58 AM
6	05/12/24	10.39 AM
7	06/12/24	11.15 AM
8	07/12/24	11.47 AM
9	08/12/24	12.17 PM
10	09/12/24	12.46 PM
11	10/12/24	1.16 PM
12	11/12/24	1.48 PM
13	12/12/24	2.25 PM
14	13/12/24	3.07 PM
15	14/12/24	3.58 PM
16	15/12/24	4.55 PM
17	16/12/24	5.58 PM
18	17/12/24	7.04 PM
19	18/12/24	8.10 PM
20	19/12/24	9.13 PM
21	20/12/24	10.15 PM
22	21/12/24	11.14 PM
23	23/12/24	12.12 AM
24	24/12/24	1.10 AM
25	25/12/24	2.09 AM
26	26/12/24	3.08 AM
27	27/12/24	4.08 AM
28	28/12/24	5.09 AM
29	29/12/24	6.08 AM
30	30/12/24	7.04 AM
1	30/12/24	5.27 PM
2	31/12/24	7.54 AM

London Time		
Calendar Day	Lunar Day	Lunar Day Start Time
01/12/24	1	6.22 AM
01/12/24	2	7.56 AM
02/12/24	3	8.57 AM
03/12/24	4	9.51 AM
04/12/24	5	10.35 AM
05/12/24	6	11.11 AM
06/12/24	7	11.40 AM
07/12/24	8	12.04 PM
08/12/24	9	12.25 PM
09/12/24	10	12.45 PM
10/12/24	11	1.05 PM
11/12/24	12	1.28 PM
12/12/24	13	1.54 PM
13/12/24	14	2.27 PM
14/12/24	15	3.08 PM
15/12/24	16	4.01 PM
16/12/24	17	5.05 PM
17/12/24	18	6.16 PM
18/12/24	19	7.29 PM
19/12/24	20	8.42 PM
20/12/24	21	9.52 PM
21/12/24	22	11.00 PM
23/12/24	23	12.07 AM
24/12/24	24	1.13 AM
25/12/24	25	2.19 AM
26/12/24	26	3.26 AM
27/12/24	27	4.34 AM
28/12/24	28	5.42 AM
29/12/24	29	6.46 AM
30/12/24	30	7.44 AM
30/12/24	1	10.27 PM
31/12/24	2	8.32 AM

You can find the description of each lunar day in the chapter "A Guide to The Moon Cycle and Lunar Days"

December may yank you from one extreme to another, giving you whiplash. The stars urge you to be adaptable and solve problems as they come. That is how you will win this battle.

Work

December has you busy at work, but this month is also a whirlwind, and you will have to put a lot of effort into getting what you want.

Business owners and managers will continue to expand their business, but this is difficult and will require a lot of elbow grease and huge investments on your part, as well.

Your relationship with colleagues in other cities or abroad is also developing, and in general, things will go well. By the end of the month, you will be talking about traveling or preparing to do just that.

Employees will see their employer continue to undergo changes, and in some cases, that may be cause for concern. If you want to leave, your job search will continue until the middle of 2025, so it is futile to try to rush things now.

Money

December is not a good time for your finances. Everyone needs money- your children, loved ones, and you might also have to make major investments in your family's needs.

Businesspeople will have to make peace with the fact that their initiatives, and business in general, will require greater resources. .

You will not end up in the red, however, and you will periodically receive some money. Expect the largest amounts on December 1, 2, 10, 11, 18, 19, 28, and 29.

Love and family

Many Scorpios might be more focused on their personal life, which will require a lot of attention this month.

Parents will continue to grapple with problems involving their children and resolving this will take time, nerves, and of course, money.

Those planning various events related to improving their home, construction, or repairs might have a hard time continuing what they started earlier. Many families might argue over money and differing views over how things should look. It is worth remembering that each person wants to do things the best they can, so there is reason to listen to one another's positions and reach a compromise.

Unmarried couples may be edging toward the brink of a breakup, and only a miracle will help them avoid it. Of course, a miracle includes love and a mutual desire to remain together.

Health

This month, you are feeling sluggish, but you have no reason to fear falling seriously ill, as long as you lead a healthy lifestyle and don't give into emotional outbursts and mood swings.

Scorpio Description

Sign. Feminine, water, fixed.

Ruler. Pluto, Mars.

Exaltation. Pluto.

Temperament. Phlegmatic, easily choleric, sarcastic.

Positive traits. Passionate, self-confident, restrained, deliberate, determined, persistent, resilient, has high self-esteem, fair, seeks recognition, is able to see an opponent's weaknesses. Richly imaginative, sensitive, a sound judge, prophetically gifted, talented.

Negative traits. Irritable, excitable, willful, critical, deceptive, rude, vindictive, insidious, passion is unbridled, excessively sexual.

Weaknesses in the body. Lower abdomen, groin, reproductive system. Organs of secretion. Bladder and renal pelvis. Gallbladder, veins.

Metal. Iron and bronze.

Minerals. For a talisman – sarder. Generally – ruby, red carnelian.

Numbers. 4, 9, 14.

Day. Tuesday.

Color. Bright red and black.

Scorpio Energy

Scorpio is a water sign ruled by Mars and Pluto. The energy of these two planets is related, and both give off sexuality, fearlessness, determination, and the ability to make decisions in extreme situations. Scorpio is capable of withstanding any battle, making the necessary changes within and rising from the ashes to a new life. Scorpio's main driving force is her incredible sexual appetite, which she gets from both Mars and Pluto. This is reflected in self-expression, love, and creativity. One's sexual energy tends to be expressed outwardly, but the water element holds it back in Scorpio, meaning that her passions live within and rarely splash out.

Astrological portrait of Scorpio

Scorpio is the most complex, mysterious, and sexiest of the Zodiac signs. It is also the strongest sign psychologically – Scorpios are considered to be innate magicians. They possess incredible intuition, and have a real talent for guessing others' thoughts, along with an ability to get those around them to speak frankly and openly. Scorpio is a sign of transformation, perfection, and rebirth. Scorpio's entire life consists of ups and downs, and the lower she falls, the higher she will climb.

Scorpio is mocking and snide, and to her, there are no secrets in human nature. Scorpio's loved ones are open books that she can easily read. Generally speaking, they strive for self-improvement, with a strong will and emotions. Few notice these emotions, however, as they burn inside, given that Scorpios are actually secretive and reserved by nature.

Scorpios are fearless and can tolerate the toughest conditions and recover from any crisis. They despise any weakness in themselves or others, and this is a constant struggle for them. By nature, Scorpios are loners and sometimes, they find it difficult to connect with others. Their personalities are very attractive and charismatic – social, active, and diplomatic, capable of controlling the powerful energy that nature has given them since birth and unwinding the collective energy to subordinate their will onto others. Scorpios are capable of achieving great things in life.

Scorpios are always consistent – in their views, in love, affection, and what they dislike. They can tend toward being overbearing or even authoritarian, but occasionally allow themselves to be manipulated. Scorpio's hardest task is coping with her passions and inner contradictions.

On one hand, Scorpios are strict (both with themselves and others), suspicious, and secretive. On the other, however, they are seeking spiritual transformation and knowledge, and are persistent, determined, fearless, and soft-hearted. This is probably why Scorpios are so attractive, too. They are capable of making a real impression and drawing everyone's attention. They are witty, but that wit can be sharp and even wound. Keep that in mind when communicating with a Scorpio.

Despite Scorpio's secrecy and distrustfulness, she can often be sincere and frank with those close to her. That trust is not easy to earn, however. This is why Scorpios tend to have a very small circle of friends they have known since childhood.

Scorpios must learn how to restrain their passions and angry outbursts. It is very difficult for them to control themselves and their temper. They need to channel that energy into something constructive, preferably creative.

How to recognize Scorpio by appearances

Outwardly, Scorpio does not appear to be particularly strong. Her strength is, after all, spiritual, rather than physical. She may appear to be rather ordinary, but there is something fascinating about her, and it not related to her external beauty.

Scorpios always look right into their partners' eyes. This is a serious, burning, and penetrating gaze. They tend to be ironic and mocking, and over time, develop characteristic crows' eyes.

Female Scorpios are easy to spot by their clothes. They love red and black (they also dye their hair these colors). Often, they prefer tight, revealing clothing, however you will rarely find a Scorpio woman who looks vulgar or tacky.

Charting Scorpio's Fate

A Scorpio's youth is a time of excitement and fateful changes. They reach success slightly later in life – after 30. Marriage is beneficial to them. This is a very sensual sign. When alone, Scorpio becomes an ascetic, channeling her sexual energy into professional endeavors.

The quality of a Scorpio's life depends on how she uses her energy. She can channel it into one of three ways.

The first path is the "Scorpian path". Scorpios here have a hard time finding their place in society. In time, they become aggressive and even dangerous. Their worst qualities take over – insidious, treacherous, a lack of empathy, unclear moral principles. They become vulnerable to many vices and dangerous addictions and get into self-destruct mode.

The second path is that of the "eagle". A Scorpio who takes this journey is aware of her power and authority. "I am so strong that I don't need to attack anyone!" is her attitude to life. Such a Scorpio becomes wise, powerful, and fair, and her energy drives her creativity. She is sociable and gifted, great company, an advocate and a fighter against injustice.

The third way is the path of the "grey lizard", or the path of least resistance. Here, Scorpio's energy does not find a worthy channel. She is dissatisfied with herself and others but does nothing to change things, becomes pessimistic, and loses her vitality.

A Guide to The Moon Cycle and Lunar Days

Since Ancient times, people have noticed that the moon has a strong influence on nature. Our Earth and everything living on it is a single living being, which is why the phases of the moon have such an effect on our health and mental state, and therefore, our lives. Remember Shakespeare and his description of Othello's jealousy in his famous tragedy:

"It is the very error of the moon, She comes more nearer Earth than she was wont And makes men mad."

If our inner rhythm is in harmony with that of the cosmos, we are able to achieve much more. People were aware of this a thousand years ago. The lunar calendar is ancient. We can find it among the ancient Sumerians (4000-3000 BC), the inhabitants of Mesopotamia, Native Americans, Hindus, and ancient Slavs. There is evidence that the Siberian Yakuts had a lunar calendar, as did the Malaysians.

Primitive tribes saw the moon as a source of fertility. Long before Christianity, the waxing moon was seen as favorable for planting new crops and starting a new business, for success and making money, while the waning moon was a sign that business would end.

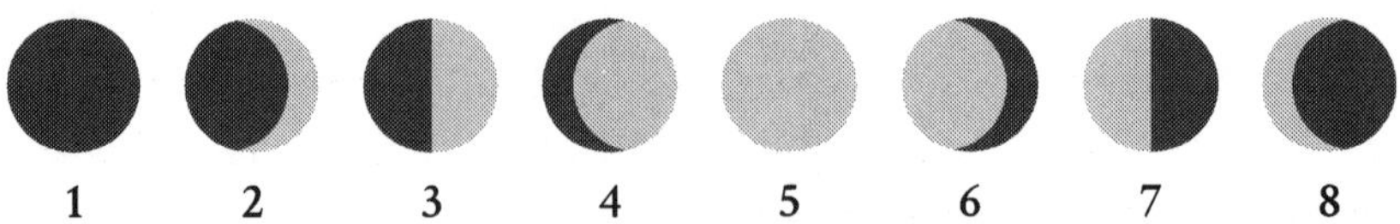

What are the phases of the moon?

- Phase 1 – new moon
- Phase 2 – waxing crescent moon
- Phase 3 – first quarter moon
- Phase 4 – waxing gibbous moon
- Phase 5 – full moon
- Phase 6 – waning gibbous moon
- Phase 7 – third quarter moon
- Phase 8 – waning crescent moon

To simplify things, we can divide the month into two phases:

- Waxing crescent moon - before the full moon
- Waning crescent moon - after the full moon

New Moon

We cannot see the new moon, as it is hidden. People might complain about feeling weak, mental imbalance, and fatigue. During this time, we want to avoid taking on too much or overdoing things. Generally, people are not very responsive and react poorly to requests, which is why it is best to look out for yourself, while not keeping your plate too full.

The new moon is a bad time for advertising – it will go unnoticed. It is not worth preparing any presentations, parties, or loud gatherings. People are feeling constrained, not very social, and sluggish.

This is also a less than ideal time for surgery, as your recovery will be slow, and the likelihood of medical error is high.

It is also difficult to get an accurate diagnosis during the new moon – diseases might seem to be hidden, and doctors might not see the real underlying cause of what ails you.

The new moon is also a bad time for dates, and sexual encounters may be dissatisfying and leave you feeling disappointed. Ancient astrologers did not advise planning a wedding night during the new moon.

Waxing Crescent Moon

It is easy to identify a waxing crescent moon. If you draw an imaginary line between the two “horns”, you should see the letter P. The waxing moon is then divided into one and two quarters.

During the first quarter moon, we need to focus on planning – setting goals and thinking of how we will set about achieving them. However, it is still a good idea to hold back a bit and not overdo things. Energy levels are still low, though they are growing along with the moon. It is still a good idea to avoid any medical procedures during this time.

The second quarter is a time for bold, decisive action. Things will come easy, and there is a greater chance of a lucky break. This is a good time for weddings, especially if the moon will be in Libra, Cancer, or Taurus. Nevertheless, it is a good idea to put off any advertising activities and public speaking until closer to the full moon, if you can.

Full Moon

During the full moon, the Earth is located between the sun and the moon. During this time, the moon is round and fully illuminated. This takes place during days 14-16 of the lunar cycle.

During the full moon, many people feel more vigorous than usual. They are emotional, sociable, and actively seeking more contact, so this may be a good time for any celebrations.

However, be careful not to drink too much – you can relax to the point that you lose control, and the consequences of that can be very unpleasant. If you are able to stick to moderation, there is no better time for a party!

The full moon is also the best time for advertising, as not only will your campaign be widely seen, people will be apt to remember it.

The full moon is also a favorable time for dates, and during this time, people are at their most open, romantic, and willing to tell each other something important that might take their relationship to the next level of trust and understanding.

Moreover, during the full moon, people feel a surge of energy, which may lead to hyperactivity, restlessness, and insomnia.

It will be harder to keep your emotions in check. You might face conflicts with friends, disasters, and accidents. During the full moon, any surgeries are **not a good idea**, as the risk of complications and bleeding is on the rise. Plastic surgery is also a bad idea, as swelling and bruises might be much worse than in another lunar phase. At the same time, the full moon is a good time to get an accurate diagnosis.

During this time, try to limit your calories and liquid intake (especially if you deal with bloating and excess weight), as your body is absorbing both calories and liquids faster during the full moon, and it can be very difficult to get rid of the weight later on.

Waning Crescent Moon

The full moon is over, and a new phase is beginning – the waning moon. This is a quieter time, when all of the jobs you started earlier are being partly or entirely completed (it all depends on the speed and scale).

Surgery will turn out much better if it is performed during the waning moon. Your recovery will be faster, and the likelihood of complications is much lower. If you have any plans to lose weight, the waning moon is the best time to do that. This is also a good time for quitting bad habits, such as smoking or cursing.

The waning moon can also be divided into the third and fourth quarters.

Third quarter - this is a favorable period, and you are able to resolve a lot of problems without conflict. People are calming down and ready to listen and take in information, while still being active. However, this is not the best time to begin any major projects, especially if you are unsure if you will be able to complete them by the start of the new lunar month.

The third quarter is a good time to get married, especially if the moon is in Cancer, Taurus, or Libra.

Fourth quarter – This is the most passive period of the lunar cycle. You are not as strong as usual. Your energy is lagging. You will be tired until reaching a new beginning. The best thing you can do as the lunar cycle comes to an end is to get things in order, and avoid anything that might get in your way at work or in personal relationships. Examine your successes and failures.

Now, let's discuss the lunar days in greater detail. For centuries, people around the world have described the influence of lunar days, and modern astrologers only add to this work, as they compare old texts to modern life.

The 1st lunar day

The first lunar day is extremely important for the rest of the lunar month. This is a much-needed day to carefully plan your activities and lay the groundwork for the rest of the lunar month. Remember that the first lunar day is not a good day for major activities, but rather for sitting down and planning things.

Avoid conflicts on this day, unless you want them to overshadow the rest of the month. Try to see the positive side of things and imagine that the lunar month will bring you good things both at work and in love. The more vividly you can imagine this, the sooner your desires will come to fruition. Perhaps it would be a good idea to jot down plans that will bring you closer to achieving your dreams. This is the best time for both manifesting and making wishes!

This is also a favorable day when it comes to seeking a new job or starting an academic program.

It is fine to go out on a date on the first lunar day, but limit any sexual contact, as your energy levels are low, and you are likely to end up disappointed.

Getting married on the first lunar day is not recommended.

Avoid getting a haircut – there are many indications that cutting your hair on the first lunar day will have a negative effect on your health and life expectancy.

Under no circumstances should you undergo any major cosmetic procedures, including plastic surgery. Energy levels are low, your skin is dull and almost stagnant. The results will not live up to your expectations, and in the worst-case scenario, you will end up looking worse than before. It is common for cosmetic procedures performed on this day to be disappointing or even useless. Even the best surgeons are less capable.

Your good dreams on the first lunar day foretell happiness and joy. Bad ones usually do not come true.

The 2nd lunar day

This is considered a lucky day, and is symbolized by a cornucopia. It is not an exaggeration to say that the second lunar day is a favorable time for both work and love. It is a time for action, and a great period to work on yourself, look for a new job, start something new, or complete any financial transaction, whether a sale or purchase. This is also a great time for creative and scientific insights, and a good time for any meeting – whether political or romantic.

Any romantic dates or sexual encounters during the second lunar day are unlikely to disappoint. This is also a good day for weddings or taking a trip with someone special.

During the second lunar day, the moon is beginning its waxing phase, which is a good time for anything you might to do nourish and restore your skin. This is a great time for any cosmetic procedures aimed at preservation, though it is best to put off any plastic surgery until the waning moon. If that is not possible, then the second lunar day is acceptable, if not ideal, and you will not run into any complications.

Folklore tells us that this is not a good day for a haircut, as that may lead to arguments with a loved one.

This is the best time for exercise – your body is in good shape, and you are able to handle new exercise regimens. If the moon happens to be in Scorpio, though, be careful.

This is a good day for anything positive, but avoid any conflicts, discussions about the status of your relationship, or litigation.

Dreams of the second lunar day are usually not prophetic.

The 3rd lunar day.

On this day, we are usually able to make out a thin sliver of the lunar crescent. It is a longstanding tradition to show money during the new month – it is believed that as the moon grows, so will your savings.

However, astrological systems around the world consider this an unlucky, unfavorable day. It is not a good idea to travel, begin any new business, or give into your bad mood.

You might run into many a lot of problems at work on this day, which will cause you a lot of anxiety. However, it is a good day to take a step back and identify and set about fixing any flaws and shortcomings. Remember that everything tends to look worse on this day than it actually is.

It is not the time to ask management for anything – you are likely to walk away disappointed, and end up unfairly reprimanded rather than receiving a promotion or raise. Instead, focus on areas of work that need to be smoothed over or studied further. It will be clear what problems you are facing, and you will easily be able to find a remedy.

Do not rush to criticize your loved ones – things may not be as they appear. “Measure twice and cut once” is your motto on this day.

This is not a good day to get married, as the couple is likely to have a turbulent, short-lived marriage.

You can schedule a cosmetic procedure for this day, but only if it is relatively minor. Plastic surgery should wait.

Do exercises as usual, without overdoing it or adding any new routines.

Dreams on this day do not mean anything.

The 4th lunar day

These are relatively neutral days, in that they are unlikely to bring anything bad, but they also will not bring you any windfalls. The fourth lunar day is symbolized by a tree of paradise, the tree of knowledge, and the choice between good and evil. Things ultimately depend on us and our final decisions.

This is a great day for anything money-related – signing contracts, agreements, or even taking on credit. There are also a lot of contradictions on this day – on one hand, we are likely to receive money, which is a good thing, but on the other, we will have to give some of it away, which is never particularly fun or pleasant. There is good reason to consider all of your opportunities and possibilities before acting.

It is not a good day to get married, as the wedding will not be as fun as you had hoped. However, the fourth lunar day is, in fact, a good day for sex and conceiving a healthy child.

Be careful on this day if you happen to engage in any physical exercise, as it is not a good idea to overeat or abuse alcohol. Take care of yourself. Any illnesses which began on this day may be extremely dangerous, if they are not dealt with immediately.

Cosmetic procedures are not contraindicated, as long as they are to preserve your appearance. Plastic surgery can be performed if you truly feel it is necessary.

However, avoid getting a haircut, as it is unlikely to grow back healthily, and will become brittle and dull. However, if the moon is in Leo, you can disregard this advice.

Dreams may turn out to be real.

The 5th lunar day

Traditionally, the fifth lunar day is one of the worst of the lunar month. It is symbolized by a unicorn. Unicorns need to be tamed, but only a virgin is capable of doing so. Many people will feel drained on this day, or frustrated with themselves, those around them, and life in general.

Try to avoid arguments- any conflicts are likely to drag out for a long time, and then you may be overcome with guilt. This advice is relevant for both work and love.

Sexual encounters may be pleasant, but this is not a good day to plan a wedding, as it is likely to lead to a marriage full of unpleasant incidents.

Do not start any new businesses, or ask those around you for favors- you may be misunderstood and rejected.

It is fine to engage in physical exercise, but if you overdo it on this day, you may injure yourself.

Your energy levels are low. Cosmetic procedures may not be effective, and avoid any plastic surgeries.

It is good if you dream something connected with the road, trips or with movement in general. A bad dream might be a sign of a health problem which should be addressed.

The 6th lunar day

The symbol of the sixth lunar day is a cloud and a crane. This is a philosophical combination that suggests that it is not worth rushing things on these days. This is a very positive, lucky day for both work and love. Creative work will be especially successful, as will any attempts at opening a new business in your field.

The sixth lunar day is a good time for resolving any financial matters. There is one limitation, however – do not give anyone a loan, as they may not pay it back. But you can certainly sponsor and support those who are more vulnerable than you.

This day is a good time to go on a trip, whether close to home or far away.

This is also a good day for dates, weddings, and marriage proposals. Remember that energy is more romantic than sexual, so it is better to give the gift of roses and a bottle of champagne than hot, passionate sex.

It is a good idea to get some exercise, but do not overdo things, though you will probably not want to, either.

Cosmetic procedures will be successful, and you can even have plastic surgery performed, so long as the moon is not in Scorpio.

It is still a good idea to avoid getting your hair cut, as you might "cut off" something good in addition to your hair.

It is better to not discuss dreams as they are usually true. Your dreams of this day can remind you of something that needs to be completed as soon as possible.

The 7th lunar day

This is also a favorable lunar day, and it is symbolized by a fighting cock, which is an Avestan deity. Avoid any aggression on this day, and instead work on yourself, spend time at home or in nature. Avoid discussing the status of your relationship with anyone, arguing, or wishing bad things on anyone. Everything will come back to haunt you, remember, silence is golden.

Business negotiations and contracts will be successful. You can find support, sponsors, and people ready to help you in both words and deeds.

Lighten up with your colleagues and subordinates. Pay attention not only to their shortcomings, but also to their skills. This is a good day for reconciliation and creating both political and romantic unions.

The seventh lunar day is good for traveling, no matter how near or far from home.

It is also a favorable time for love and marriage.

Exercise moderately, and any plastic surgeries will go very smoothly, as long as the moon is not in Scorpio.

Dreams of this day may become a reality.

The 8th lunar day

The symbol for this day is a Phoenix, which symbolizes eternal rebirth and renewal, because this day is a great time for changes in all areas of your life. Your energy is likely to be high, and you want to do something new and unusual. This is a good time to look for a new job or begin studying something. Any out-of-the-box thinking is welcome, along with shaking things up a bit in order to improve your life.

However, avoid any financial transactions, as you may incur losses.

Avoid aggression. You can share your opinion by presenting well-founded arguments and facts, instead.

The phoenix rises from the ashes, so this is a good time to be careful with electrical appliances and fire in general. The risk of housefires is high.

Avoid any major financial transactions on the eighth day, as you may end up facing a series of complications. You can pay people their salaries, as this is unlikely to be a large sum.

This is a good day for weddings, but only if you and your future spouse are restless, creative souls and hope to achieve personal development through your marriage.

Any cosmetic procedures and plastic surgeries will go well today, as they are related to rebirth and renewal. Surgeons may find that they are true artists on this day!

You can try to change your hairstyle and get a fashionable haircut on this day.

You can trust your dreams seen on this day.

The 9th lunar day

The ninth lunar day is not particularly auspicious, and is even referred to as "Satan's" day. You may be overcome with doubt, suspicions, even depression and conflicts.

Your self-esteem will suffer, so don't overdo things physically, and avoid overeating or abusing alcohol.

This is a negative day for any business deals, travel, or financial transactions.

This is a particularly bad day for any events, so keep your head down at work and avoid any new initiatives.

It is better to avoid getting married on "Satan's" day, as the marriage will not last very long. Avoid sex, as well, but you can take care of your partner, listen them, and support them however they need.

Any cosmetic procedures will not have a lasting effect, and avoid any plastic surgery. A haircut will not turn out as you hoped.

Dreams of this day are usually prophetic.

The 10th lunar day

This is one of the luckiest days of the lunar month. It is symbolized by a spring, mushroom, or phallus. This is a time for starting a new business, learning new things, and creating.

The 10th lunar day is particularly lucky for business. Networking and financial transactions will be a success and bring hope. This is an ideal time for changing jobs, shifting your business tactics, and other renewals.

This is a perfect time for people in creative fields and those working in science, who may come up with incredible ideas that will bring many successful returns.

This is a very successful day for building a family and proposing marriage. This is a good time for celebrations and communication, so plan parties, meet with friends, and plan a romantic date.

One of the symbols for this day is a phallus, so sexual encounters are likely to be particularly satisfying.

The 10th lunar day is the best time to begin repairs, buying furniture, and items for home improvement.

You can exercise vigorously, and cosmetic procedures and plastic surgery will be very effective.

Dreams of this day will not come true.

The 11th lunar day

This is one of the best lunar days, and seen as the pinnacle of the lunar cycle. People are likely to be energetic, enthusiastic, and ready to move forward toward their goals.

The 11th lunar day is very successful for any financial transactions or business deals and meetings.

You might actively make yourself known, approach management to discuss a promotion, or look for a new job. This is an auspicious time for advertising campaigns, performances, and holding meetings.

Any trips planned will be a great success, whether near or far from home.

Romantic relationships are improving, sex is harmonious, and very desired.

Weddings held on this day will be fun, and the marriage will be a source of joy and happiness.

Exercise is a great idea, and you might even beat your own personal record.

This is an ideal time for any cosmetic procedures, but any more serious plastic surgeries might lead to a lot of bruising and swelling.

A haircut will turn out as you had hoped, and you can experiment a bit with your appearance.

You can ignore dreams of this day – usually they do not mean anything.

The 12th lunar day

This day is symbolized by the Grail and a heart. As we move closer to the full moon, our emotions are at their most open. During this time, if you ask someone for something, your request will be heeded. This is a day of faith, goodness, and divine revelations.

For business and financial transactions, this is not the most promising day. However, if you help others on this day, your good deeds are sure to come back to you.

This is a day for reconciliation, so do not try to explain your relationships, as no one is at fault, and it is better to focus on yourself, anyway.

Avoid weddings and sex on this day, but if you want to do what your partner asks, there is no better time.

Many may feel less than confident and cheerful during this day, so take it easy when working out. Avoid overeating, stay hydrated, and avoid alcohol.

The 12th lunar day is not the best for getting married or having sex, but the stars would welcome affection and a kind word.

Avoid getting a haircut, or any plastic surgeries. This is a neutral day for minor cosmetic procedures.

Nearly all dreams will come true.

The 13th lunar day

This day is symbolized by Samsara, the wheel of fate, which is very erratic and capable of moving in any direction. This is why the 13th lunar day is full of contradictions. In Indian traditions, this day is compared to a snake eating its own tail. This is a day for paying off old debts and returning to unfinished business.

Avoid beginning any new business on this day. It is preferable to finish old tasks and proofread your work. Information you receive on this day may not be reliable and must be verified.

It is worth resolving financial problems very carefully, and avoid arguments and conflict.

Do not change jobs on this day or go to a new place for the first time. Do not sit at home alone, though, go see old friends, parents, or older family members.

Minor cosmetic procedures are welcome on this day, but avoid any plastic surgery, as you may experience major swelling and bruising. Avoid any haircuts, too.

As a rule, all dreams will come true.

The 14th lunar day

It's a full moon! The 14th lunar day is one of the happiest, and it is symbolized by the trumpet. Pay attention – you may run into new, much-needed information. Networking will be successful, and you can confidently sign agreements, meet with people, and attend fun gatherings or other leisure activities. This is one of the best days for advertising, performances, and concerts, and those working in creative professions should keep this in mind, as should those who work in politics. Do not sit in place on this day – you need to get out and see others, make new connections, and try to be visible.

This is one of the best days for communication with and making requests from management, as your initiatives will be noticed and welcome. You might talk about a promotion, raise, or something similarly related to professional growth.

Couples will see their relationship is moving along well on this day, and it is also a good day for getting married.

Any sex on this day will be vigorous and memorable for a long time. The full moon is the best time for conceiving a child.

Any cosmetic procedures will be effective, but avoid any major changes to your appearance, as there is a high likelihood of bleeding and bruising. A haircut will turn out well.

Your dreams of this day will be more or less doubtful.

The 15th lunar day

It's a full moon! This day is symbolized by a serpent of fire. This is the energy peak of the entire lunar cycle, and a lot will depend on where you are focusing your energy.

You might face a lot of temptations on this day, for example, you might tell someone else's secret or your own to others, and come to regret it for a long time. The stars suggest exercising restraint in both your words and actions, as the 15th day of the lunar cycle is a day of deception and weaknesses.

This is a very active time, and many people might take unnecessary risks. This is not the best day for signing any agreements or contracts. For any performances, concerts, or advertising, however, this is one of the best days of the month.

You can get married on the 15th day, but only if you know each other well and have carefully considered your partnership, without any hasty decisions. This is also a favorable day for a second marriage.

Your romantic relationship is looking wonderful – you are on cloud 9, writing poetry, and deeply convinced of how right your partner is for you – and they feel the same way. It is important that this does not suddenly lead to an abrupt disappointment.

Avoid getting any haircuts on the 15th day of the month, as you may end up with a headache.

Conservative cosmetic procedures and creams will be very effective, but avoid any injections or plastic surgery today. Bleeding, swelling, and bruising are all but guaranteed.

Dreams on the 15th day nearly always come true.

The 16th lunar day

This day is symbolized by a dove. The full moon is over, and the moon is now in its waning phase. Usually, after the turbulent days of the full moon, people feel a bit under the weather. They are not cheerful, and want to avoid excess worry and give themselves a chance to breathe.

Don't ignore your body's wishes, take it easy with physical activities, and take some time for yourself. You might spend time in nature, in the forest, or at a country home.

The 16th day of the lunar month is a time for moderation in all areas – your behavior, eating, and even in your clothes. If you overate during the full moon period, now is the time to diet a bit or at least avoid fatty foods and meat.

This is not a promising day for resolving any financial matters. Keep your documents in order and get ready for any future meetings, instead. If you help a loved one, your good deed will come back 100 times over.

Avoid getting married today, as well as sex.

Cosmetic procedures are likely to be a success, especially if they are related to cleansing your skin, but it is best to avoid any plastic surgery or injections. Your body is not ready to accept them. A haircut will turn out as you hoped.

Any dreams are likely to come true, but that also depends on a correct interpretation.

The 17th lunar day

This day is represented by a vine and bell. It is a happy day and both successful and fun-filled. It is also a good time for negotiations, concluding small business deals, shaking up staffing, and creativity. However, you should keep in mind that the 17th day is only favorable for minor business, and you should avoid starting any major events.

Avoid any major financial transactions on this day. Do not give anyone money as a loan or borrow anything yourself, either.

Any travel, whether for business or pleasure, is likely to be a success.

The 17th day is a great time to get married, and an ideal day for dates. Any sexual encounters will bring you happiness and joy.

Avoid getting your hair cut on this day, but cosmetic procedures and plastic surgery will be a success. Women will look better than usual.

Your dreams are likely to come true in three days.

The 18th lunar day

This day is represented by a mirror. It is a difficult, and generally unpromising day, too. Just as the mirror reflects our imperfections back to us, we need to remember that moderation and modesty are key.

The 18th day is not a favorable time for any business meetings or financial transactions. You can, however work on jobs you already began. It is, however, a positive day for those who work in research or the creative fields.

Your motto of the day is to keep a cool head when it comes to your opportunities and the opportunities of those around you. This is relevant for both work and romantic relationships. It is not a good time to criticize others – any conflicts or arguments may lead to lasting consequences, which you do not need.

Avoid getting married on this day, as well as sexual encounters, which are likely to be disappointing. It is a good time to take a trip together, which will only be good for your relationship.

Avoid getting your hair cut, though this is a relatively neutral day for a haircut, which might turn out well, and though it will not exceed your expectations, it will also not leave you upset. Avoid any plastic surgeries.

Dreams on this day will come true.

The 19th lunar day

This is a very difficult day and it is represented by a spider. The energy is complicated, if not outright dangerous. Don't panic or get depressed, though – this is a test of your strength, and if you are able to hold onto all you have achieved. This is relevant for both work and love. On the 19th day, you should avoid taking any trips.

The energy of the 19th lunar day is very unfavorable for beginning any major projects, and business in general. Work on what you started earlier, get your affairs in order, think over your ideas and emotions, and check to make sure that everything you have done hitherto is living up to your expectations. Do not carry out any financial transactions or take out any loans – do not loan anyone else money, either. Do not ask your managers for anything as they are unlikely to listen to what you have to say, and make judgments instead.

This is a day when you might face outright deception, so do not take any risks and ignore rumors. Do not work on anything related to real estate or legal matters.

This is a very hard time for people with an unbalanced psyche, as they may experience sudden exacerbations or even suicidal ideations.

This is a very unlucky day to get married. Sexual encounters might be disappointing and significantly worsen your relationship.

Avoid any haircuts or cosmetic procedures or surgeries.

Your dreams of this day will come true.

The 20th lunar day

This is also a difficult day, though less so than the 19th. It is represented by an eagle. This is a good time to work on your own development and spiritual growth, by speaking to a psychologist or astrologer.

Avoid pride, anger, arrogance, and envy.

The 20th lunar day is a good time for people who are active and decisive. They will be able to easily overcome any obstacles, flying over them just like an eagle. If you have to overcome your own fears, you will be able to do so – don't limit yourself, and you will see that there is nothing to be afraid of. It is a good day for any financial transactions, signing contracts, and reaching agreements, as well as networking.

The 20th lunar day is a favorable time for those who work in the creative fields, as they will be able to dream up the idea that will open up a whole host of new possibilities. Avoid conflicts – they may ruin your relationship with a lot of people, and it will not be easy to come back from that.

This is a lucky day for getting married, but only if you have been with your partner for several years, now. Sexual encounters will not be particularly joyful, but they also will not cause you any problems.

Avoid getting your hair cut, but you can certainly get it styled. The 20th lunar day is a good day for those who are looking to lose weight. You will be able to do so quickly, and it will be easy for you to follow a diet.

Cosmetic procedures will be a success, as will any plastic surgeries.

Pay attention to dreams of this day as they are likely to come true.

The 21st lunar day

This is one of the most successful days of the lunar month, and it is symbolized by a herd of horses – imagine energy, strength, speed, and bravery. Everything you think up will happen quickly, and you will be able to easily overcome obstacles. A mare is not only brave but also an honest animal, so you will only experience this luck if you remember that honesty is always the best policy.

This is also a favorable day for business. Reaching new agreements and signing contracts, or dealing with foreign partners – it is all likely to be a success. Any financial issues will be resolved successfully.

Those in the creative world will be able to show off their talent and be recognized for their work. Anyone involved in the performing arts can expect success, luck, and recognition. A galloping herd of horses moves quickly, so you might transition to a new job, move to a new apartment, or go on a business trip or travel with your better half.

The 21st lunar day is one of the best to get married or have a sexual encounter.

This is a great time for athletes, hunters, and anyone who likes adventurous activities.

But for criminals and thieves, this is not a lucky or happy day – they will quickly be brought to justice.

Any haircuts or cosmetic procedures are likely to be a huge success and bring both beauty and happiness. You will recover quickly after any surgeries, perhaps without any swelling or bruising at all.

Dreams tend to not be reliable.

The 22nd lunar day

This day will be strange and contradictory. It is symbolized by the elephant Ganesha. According to Indian mythology, Ganesha is the patron saint of hidden knowledge. so this is a favorable day for anyone who is trying to learn more about the world and ready to find the truth, though this is often seen as a hopeless endeavor. This is a day for philosophers and wisemen and women. However, it is an inauspicious day for business, and unlikely to lead to resolving financial issues, signing contracts, agreements, or beginning new projects. You can expect trouble at work.

For creative people, and new employees, this is a successful day.

This is a good day for apologies and reconciliation.

Avoid getting married, though you can feel free to engage in sexual encounters.

For haircuts and cosmetic procedures, this is a fantastic day. Surgeries will also turn out, as long as the moon is not in Scorpio.

Dreams will come true.

The 23rd lunar day

This is a challenging day represented by a crocodile, which is a very aggressive animal. This is a day of strong energy, but it is also adventurous and tough. Your main task is to focus your energy in the right direction. There may be accidents, arguments, conflicts, fights, and violence, which is why it is important to strive for balance and calm.

Keep a close eye on your surroundings – there may be traitors or people who do not wish you well, so be careful.

However, this is still a favorable day for business – many problems will be resolved successfully. You are able to sign contracts and receive credit successfully, as long as you remain active and decisive in what you do.

This is not a day for changing jobs or working on real estate transactions or legal proceedings. This is not a favorable day for traveling, no matter how near or far you plan on going.

This is not a promising day to get married – things may end in conflict, if not an all-out brawl.

Sexual relations are not off the table, as long as the couple trusts one another.

Haircuts or cosmetic procedures will not turn out as you had hoped, so avoid them.

Dreams during this lunar day usually mean something opposite of what awaits you, so you can disregard them.

The 24th lunar day

This is a neutral, calm day that is symbolized by a bear. It is favorable for forgiveness and reconciliation.

This is also a good day for learning new things, reading, self-development, and taking time to relax in nature.

This is a great day for any type of financial activity, conferences, academic meetings, and faraway travel.

The 24th lunar day is a good time for love and getting married, as any marriage will be strong and lasting.

Cosmetic procedures and plastic surgery will be a success, and you can expect a speedy recovery.

Avoid getting a haircut on this day, however, as your hair will likely thin and grow back slowly.

Dreams of this lunar day are usually connected with your personal life.

The 25th lunar day

This is still another quiet day, symbolized by a turtle.

Just like a turtle, this is not a day to rush, and it is best to sit down and take stock of your life. This is a good time for resolving any personal problems, as the moon's energy makes it possible for you to calm down and find the right path.

This is also not a bad day for business. It is believed that any business you begin on this day is sure to be a success. This is especially the case for trade and any monetary activities.

The 25th lunar day is not a good day to get married, especially if the couple is very young.

This is a neutral day for sexual encounters, as the moon is waning, energy is low, so the decision is yours.

Avoid any cosmetic procedures, except those for cleansing your skin. This is not a favorable day for haircuts or plastic surgery – unless the moon is in Libra or Leo.

You can have a prophetic dream on this day.

The 26th lunar day

The 26th lunar day is full of contradictions and complicated. It is represented by a toad.

It is not time to start or take on something new, as nothing good will come of it. Avoid any major purchases, as you will later come to see that your money was wasted. The best thing you can do on this day is stay at home and watch a good movie or read a good book.

Avoid traveling on this day, as it may not turn out well.

The 26th lunar day is a negative day for any business negotiations and starting new businesses. Do not complete any business deals or financial transactions. Your colleagues may be arguing, and your managers may be dissatisfied. But if you have decided to leave your job, there is no better time to do so.

This is not a good day to get married, as both partners' expectations may fall flat, and they will soon be disappointed.

The waning moon carries a negative charge, so avoid any haircuts and surgeries, though you can get cosmetic procedures if they are relatively minor.

Your dreams will come true.

The 27th lunar day

The 27th lunar day is one of the best days of the month, and it is represented by a ship. You can boldly start any new business, which is sure to be promising. This is a great day for students, teachers, and learning new things. Any information that comes to you on this day may be extremely valuable and useful to you.

The 27th day is good for communication and travel, whether near or far from home, and no matter whether it is for work or pleasure.

This is also a good day for any professional activities or financial transactions. If there are people around you who need help, you must support them, as your good deeds will come back 100-fold.

Romantic dates will go well, though any weddings should be quiet and subdued. This is a particularly good day for older couples or second marriages.

The waning moon means that hair will grow back very slowly, but in general, you can expect a haircut to turn out well. This is a great day for plastic surgery or cosmetic procedures, as the results will be pleasing, and you will have a speedy recovery, without any bruising or swelling, most of the time.

However, beware if the moon is in Scorpio on this day – that is not a good omen for any plastic surgery.

Do not pay any attention to dreams on this day.

The 28th lunar day

This is another favorable day in the waning moon cycle, and it is represented by a lotus. This is a day of wisdom and spiritual awakening. If possible, spend part of the day in nature. It is important to take stock of the last month and decide what you need to do during its two remaining days.

This is a good time for any career development, changing jobs, conducting business, decision-making, and signing agreements, as well as going on a trip. You might conclude any business deal, hold negotiations, work with money and securities.

This is also a good day for any repairs or improvements around your home or apartment.

Any weddings today should be subdued and modest, and restricted to family members only. A loud, raucous wedding might not turn out very well. Your hair will grow slowly, but any haircuts will turn out very elegant and stylish. Cosmetic procedures and surgeries are not contraindicated. You will recover quickly with little bruising and swelling.

Do not take any dreams too seriously.

The 29th lunar day

This is one of the most difficult days of the lunar month, and it is considered a Satanic day, unlucky for everyone and everything. It is symbolized by an octopus.

This is a dark day, and many will feel melancholy, depression, and a desire to simply be left alone. This is a day full of conflict and injuries, so be careful everywhere and with everyone. If you can, avoid any travel, and be particularly careful when handling any sharp objects. Do not engage in any business negotiations, sign any contracts, or take part in any networking.

Astrologers believe that anything you start on this day will completely fall apart. For once and for all, get rid of things that are impeding you from living your life. This is a good time to avoid people who you do find unpleasant.

This is also a time for fasting and limitations for everyone. Do not hold any celebrations, weddings, or have sexual relations – these events may not turn out as you hoped, and instead bring you nothing but suffering and strife.

Avoid getting a haircut, as well, as it will not make you look more beautiful and your hair will come back lifeless and dull. Cosmetic procedures can go ahead, but avoid any surgeries.

Dreams are likely to be true.

The 30th lunar day

There is not always a 30th lunar day, as some lunar months have only 29 days. This day is represented by a swan. The 30th lunar day is usually very short, and sometimes, it lasts less than an hour. This is a time for forgiveness and calm.

You might take stock of the last month, while also avoiding anything you do not need around you. Pay back loans, make donations, reconcile with those who recently offended you, and stop speaking to people who cause you suffering.

This is a good time for tying up loose ends, and many astrologers believe that it is also a good day to start new business.

However, avoid celebrations or weddings on this day. Spouses will either not live long, or they will quickly grow apart.

Do not get a haircut on this day, though cosmetic procedures are possible, as long as you avoid any surgeries.

Dreams promise happiness and should come true.

A Guide to Zodiac Compatibility

Often, when we meet a person, we get a feeling that they are good and we take an instant liking to them. Another person, however, gives us immediate feelings of distrust, fear and hostility. Is there an astrological reason why people say that 'the first impression is the most accurate'? How can we detect those who will bring us nothing but trouble and unhappiness?

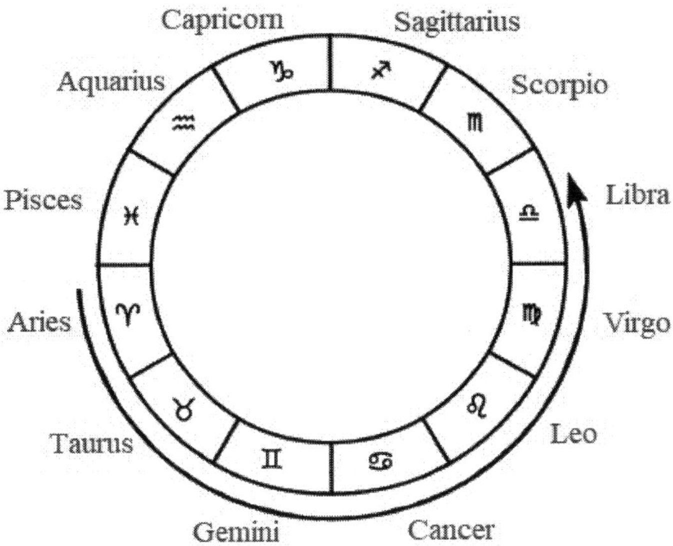

Without going too deeply into astrological subtleties unfamiliar to some readers, it is possible to determine the traits according to which friendship, love or business relationships will develop.

Let's begin with problematic relationships - our most difficult are with our **8th sign**. For example, for Aries the 8th sign is Scorpio, for Taurus it is Sagittarius and so on. Finding your 8th sign is easy; assume your own sign to be first (see above Figure) and then move eight signs counter clockwise around the Zodiac circle. This is also how the other signs (fourth, ninth and so on) that we mention are to be found.

Ancient astrologers variously referred to the 8th sign as the symbol of death, of destruction, of fated love or unfathomable attraction. In astrological terms, this pair is called 'master and slave' or 'boa constrictor and rabbit', with the role of 'master' or 'boa constrictor' being played by our 8th sign.

This relationship is especially difficult for politicians and business people.

We can take the example of a recent political confrontation in the USA. Hilary Clinton is a Scorpio while Donald Trump is a Gemini - her 8th sign. Even though many were certain that Clinton would be elected President, she lost.

To take another example, Hitler was a Taurus and his opponents – Stalin and Churchill - were both of his 8th sign, Sagittarius. The result of their confrontation is well known. Interestingly, the Russian Marshals who dealt crushing military blows to Hitler and so helped end the Third Reich - Konstantin Rokossovsky and Georgy Zhukov - were also Sagittarian, Hitler's 8th sign.

In another historical illustration, Lenin was also a Taurus. Stalin was of Lenin's 8th sign and was ultimately responsible for the downfall and possibly death of his one-time comrade-in-arms.

Business ties with those of our 8th sign are hazardous as they ultimately lead to stress and loss; both financial and moral. So, do not tangle with your 8th sign and never fight with it - your chances of winning are remote!

Such relationships are very interesting in terms of love and romance, however. We are magnetically attracted to our 8th sign and even though it may be very intense physically, it is very difficult for family life;

'Feeling bad when together, feeling worse when apart'.

As an example, let us take the famous lovers - George Sand who was Cancer and Alfred de Musset who was Sagittarius. Cancer is the 8th sign for Sagittarius, and the story of their crazy two-year love affair was the subject of much attention throughout France. Critics and writers were divided into 'Mussulist' and 'Sandist' camps; they debated fiercely about who was to blame for the sad ending to their love story - him or her. It's hard to imagine the energy needed to captivate the public for so long, but that energy was destructive for the couple. Passion raged in their hearts, but neither of them was able to comprehend their situation.

Georges Sand wrote to Musset, "*I don't love you anymore, and I will always adore you. I don't want you anymore, and I can't do without you. It seems that nothing but a heavenly lightning strike can heal me by destroying me. Good-bye! Stay or go, but don't say that I am not suffering. This is the only thing that can make me suffer even more, my love, my life, my blood! Go away, but kill me, leaving.*" Musset replied only in brief, but its power surpassed Sand's tirade, "*When you embraced me, I felt something that is still bothering me, making it impossible for me to approach another woman.*" These two people loved each other passionately and for two years lived together in a powder keg of passion, hatred and treachery.

When someone enters into a romantic liaison with their 8th sign, there will be no peace; indeed, these relationships are very attractive to those who enjoy the edgy, the borderline and, in the Dostoevsky style, the melodramatic. The first to lose interest in the relationship is, as a rule, the 8th sign.

If, by turn of fate, our child is born under our 8th sign, they will be very different from us and, in some ways, not live up to our expectations. It may be best to let them choose their own path.

In business and political relationships, the combination with our **12th sign** is also a complicated one.

We can take two political examples. Angela Merkel is a Cancer while Donald Trump is a Gemini - her 12th sign. This is why their relations are strained and complicated and we can even perhaps assume that the American president will achieve his political goals at her expense. Boris Yeltsin (Aquarius) was the 12th sign to Mikhail Gorbachev (Pisces) and it was Yeltsin who managed to dethrone the champion of Perestroika.

Even ancient astrologers noticed that our relationships with our 12th signs can never develop evenly; it is one of the most curious and problematic combinations. They are our hidden enemies and they seem to be digging a hole for us; they ingratiate themselves with us, discover our innermost secrets. As a result, we become bewildered and make mistakes when we deal with them. Among the Roman emperors murdered by members of their entourage, there was an interesting pattern - all the murderers were the 12th sign of the murdered.

We can also see this pernicious effect in Russian history: the German princess Alexandra (Gemini) married the last Russian Tsar Nicholas II (Taurus) - he was her 12th sign and brought her a tragic death. The wicked genius Grigory Rasputin (Cancer) made friends with Tsarina Alexandra, who was his 12th sign, and was murdered as a result of their odd friendship. The weakness of Nicholas II was exposed, and his authority reduced after the death of the economic and social reformer Pyotr Stolypin, who was his 12th sign. Thus, we see a chain of people whose downfall was brought about by their 12th sign.

So, it makes sense to be cautious of your 12th sign, especially if you have business ties. Usually, these people know much more about us than we want them to and they will often reveal our secrets for personal gain if it suits them. However, the outset of these relationships is, as a rule, quite normal - sometimes the two people will be friends, but sooner or later one will betray the other one or divulge a secret; inadvertently or not.

In terms of romantic relationships, our 12th sign is gentle, they take care of us and are tender towards us. They know our weaknesses well but accept them with understanding. It is they who guide us, although sometimes almost imperceptibly. Sexual attraction is usually strong.

For example, Meghan Markle is a Leo, the 12th sign for Prince Harry, who is a Virgo. Despite Queen Elizabeth II being lukewarm about the match, Harry's love was so strong that they did marry.

If a child is our 12th sign, it later becomes clear that they know all our secrets, even those that they are not supposed to know. It is very difficult to control them as they do everything in their own way.

Relations with our **7th sign** are also interesting. They are like our opposite; they have something to learn from us while we, in turn, have something to learn from them. This combination, in business and personal relationships, can be very positive and stimulating provided that both partners are quite intelligent and have high moral standards but if not, constant misunderstandings and challenges follow. Marriage or co-operation with the 7th sign can only exist as the union of two fully-fledged individuals and in this case love, significant business achievements and social success are possible.

However, the combination can be not only interesting, but also quite complicated.

An example is Angelina Jolie, a Gemini, and Brad Pitt, a Sagittarius. This is a typical bond with a 7th sign - it's lively and interesting, but rather stressful. Although such a couple may quarrel and even part from time to time, never do they lose interest in each other.

This may be why this combination is more stable in middle-age when there is an understanding of the true nature of marriage and partnership. In global, political terms, this suggests a state of eternal tension - a cold war - for example between Yeltsin (Aquarius) and Bill Clinton (Leo).

Relations with our **9th sign** are very good; they are our teacher and advisor - one who reveals things we are unaware of and our relationships with them very often involve travel or re-location. The combination can lead to spiritual growth and can be beneficial in terms of business.

Although, for example, Trump and Putin are political opponents, they can come to an understanding and even feel a certain sympathy for each other because Putin is a Libra while Trump is a Gemini, his 9th sign.

This union is also quite harmonious for conjugal and romantic relationships.

We treat our **3rd sign** somewhat condescendingly. They are like our younger siblings; we teach them and expect them to listen attentively. Our younger brothers and sisters are more often than not born under this sign. In terms of personal and sexual relationships, the union is not very inspiring and can end quickly, although this is not always the case. In terms of business, it is fairly average as it often connects partners from different cities or countries.

We treat our **5th sign** as a child and we must take care of them accordingly. The combination is not very good for business, however, since our 5th sign triumphs over us in terms of connections and finances, and thereby gives us very little in return save for love or sympathy. However, they are very good for family and romantic relationships, especially if the 5th sign is female. If a child is born as a 5th sign to their parents, their relationship will be a mutually smooth, loving and understanding one that lasts a lifetime.

Our **10th sign** is a born leader. Depending on the spiritual level of those involved, both pleasant and tense relations are possible; the relationship is often mutually beneficial in the good times but mutually disruptive in the bad times. In family relations, our 10th sign always tries to lead and will do so according to their intelligence and upbringing.

Our **4th sign** protects our home and can act as a sponsor to strengthen our financial or moral positions. Their advice should be heeded in all cases as it can be very effective, albeit very unobtrusive. If a woman takes this role, the relationship can be long and romantic, since all the spouse's wishes are usually met one way or another. Sometimes, such couples achieve great social success; for instance, Hilary Clinton, a Scorpio is the 4th sign to Bill Clinton, a Leo. On the other hand, if the husband is the 4th sign for his wife, he tends to be henpecked. There is often a strong sexual attraction. Our 4th sign can improve our living conditions and care for us in a parental way. If a child is our 4th sign, they are close to us and support us affectionately.

Relations with our **11th sign** are often either friendly or patronizing; we treat them reverently, while they treat us with friendly condescension. Sometimes, these relationships develop in an 'older brother' or 'high-ranking friend' sense; indeed, older brothers and sisters are often our 11th sign. In terms of personal and sexual relationships, our 11th sign is always inclined to enslave us. This tendency is most clearly manifested in such alliances as Capricorn and Pisces or Leo and Libra. A child who is the 11th sign to their parents will achieve greater success than their parents, but this will only make the parents proud.

Our **2nd sign** should bring us financial or other benefits; we receive a lot from them in both our business and our family life. In married couples, the 2nd sign usually looks after the financial situation for the benefit of the family. Sexual attraction is strong.

Our **6th sign** is our 'slave'; we always benefit from working with them and it's very difficult for them to escape our influence. In the event of hostility, especially if they have provoked the conflict, they receive a powerful retaliatory strike. In personal relations, we can almost destroy them by making them dance to our tune. For example, if a husband doesn't allow his wife to work or there are other adverse family circumstances, she gradually becomes lost as an individual despite being surrounded by care. This is the best-case scenario; worse outcomes are possible. Our 6th sign has a strong sexual attraction to us because we are the fatal 8th sign for them; we cool down quickly, however, and often make all kinds of demands. If the relationship with our 6th sign is a long one, there is a danger that routine, boredom and stagnation will ultimately destroy the relationship. A child born under our 6th sign needs particularly careful handling as they can feel fear or embarrassment when communicating with us. Their health often needs increased attention and we should also remember that they are very different from us emotionally.

Finally, we turn to relations with **our own sign**. Scorpio with Scorpio and Cancer with Cancer get along well, but in most other cases, however, our own sign is of little interest to us as it has a similar energy. Sometimes, this relationship can develop as a rivalry, either in business or in love.

There is another interesting detail - we are often attracted to one particular sign. For example, a man's wife and mistress often have the same sign. If there is confrontation between the two, the stronger character displaces the weaker one. As an example, Prince Charles is a Scorpio, while both Princess Diana and Camilla Parker Bowles were born under the sign of Cancer. Camilla was the more assertive and became dominant.

Of course, in order to draw any definitive conclusions, we need an individually prepared horoscope, but the above always, one way or another, manifests itself.

Love Description of Zodiac Signs

We know that human sexual behavior has been studied at length. Entire libraries have been written about it, with the aim of helping us understand ourselves and our partners. But is that even possible? It may not be; no matter how smart we are, when it comes to love and sex, there is always an infinite amount to learn. But we have to strive for perfection, and astrology, with its millennia of research, twelve astrological types, and twelve zodiac signs, may hold the key. Below, you will find a brief and accurate description of each zodiac sign's characteristics in love, for both men and women.

Men

ARIES

Aries men are not particularly deep or wise, but they make up for it in sincerity and loyalty. They are active, even aggressive lovers, but a hopeless romantic may be lurking just below the surface. Aries are often monogamous and chivalrous men, for whom there is only one woman (of course, in her absence, they can sleep around with no remorse). If the object of your affection is an Aries, be sure to give him a lot of sex, and remember that for an Aries, when it comes to sex, anything goes. Aries cannot stand women who are negative or disheveled. They need someone energetic, lively, and to feel exciting feelings of romance.

The best partner for an Aries is Cancer, Sagittarius, or Leo. Aquarius can also be a good match, but the relationship will be rather friendly in nature. Partnering with a Scorpio or Taurus will be difficult, but they can be stimulating lovers for an Aries. Virgos are good business contacts, but a poor match as lovers or spouses.

TAURUS

A typical Taurean man is warm, friendly, gentle, and passionate, even if he doesn't always show it. He is utterly captivated by the beauty of the female body, and can find inspiration in any woman. A Taurus has such excess physical and sexual prowess, that to him, sex is a way to relax and calm down. He is the most passionate and emotional lover of the Zodiac, but he expects his partner to take the initiative, and if she doesn't, he will easily find someone else. Taureans rarely divorce, and are true to the end – if not sexually, at least spiritually. They are secretive, keep their cards close, and may have secret lovers. If a Taurus does not feel a deep emotional connection with someone, he won't be shy to ask her friends for their number. He prefers a voluptuous figure over an athletic or skinny woman.

The best partners for a Taurus are Cancer, Virgo, Pisces, or Scorpio. Sagittarius can show a Taurus real delights in both body and spirit, but they are unlikely to make it down the aisle. They can have an interesting relationship with an Aquarius – these signs are very different, but sometimes can spend their lives together. They might initially feel attracted to an Aries, before rejecting her.

GEMINI

The typical Gemini man is easygoing and polite. He is calm, collected, and analytical. For a Gemini, passion is closely linked to intellect, to the point that they will try to find an explanation for their actions before carrying them out. But passion cannot be explained, which scares a Gemini, and they begin jumping from one extreme to the other. This is why you will find more bigamists among Geminis than any other sign of the Zodiac. Sometimes, Gemini men even have two families, or divorce and marry several times throughout the course of their lives. This may be because they simply can't let new and interesting experiences pass them by. A Gemini's wife or lover needs to be smart, quick, and always looking ahead. If she isn't, he will find a new object for his affection.

Aquarians, Libras, and Aries make good partners for a Gemini. A Sagittarius can be fascinating for him, but they will not marry before he reaches middle age, as both partners will be fickle while they are younger. A Gemini and Scorpio are likely to be a difficult match, and the Gemini will try to wriggle out of the Scorpio's tight embrace. A Taurus will be an exciting sex partner, but their partnership won't be for long, and the Taurus is often at fault.

CANCER

Cancers tend to be deep, emotional individuals, who are both sensitive and highly sexual. Their charm is almost mystical, and they know how to use it. Cancers may be the most promiscuous sign of the Zodiac, and open to absolutely anything in bed. Younger Cancers look for women who are more mature, as they are skilled lovers. As they age, they look for someone young enough to be their own daughter, and delight in taking on the role of a teacher. Cancers are devoted to building a family and an inviting home, but once they achieve that goal, they are likely to have a wandering eye. They will not seek moral justification, as they sincerely believe it is simply something everyone does. Their charm works in such a way that women are deeply convinced they are the most important love in a Cancer's life, and that circumstances are the only thing preventing them from being together. Remember that a Cancer man is a master manipulator, and will not be yours unless he is sure you have throngs of admirers. He loves feminine curves, and is turned on by exquisite fragrances. Cancers don't end things with old lovers, and often go back for a visit after a breakup. Another type of Cancer is rarer – a faithful friend, and up for anything in order to provide for his wife and children. He is patriotic and a responsible worker.

Scorpios, Pisces, and other Cancers are a good match. A Taurus can make for a lasting relationship, as both signs place great value on family and are able to get along with one another. A Sagittarius will result in fights and blowouts from the very beginning, followed by conflicts and breakups. The Sagittarius will suffer the most. Marriage to an Aries isn't off the table, but it won't last very long.

LEO

A typical Leo is handsome, proud, and vain, with a need to be the center of attention at all times. They often pretend to be virtuous, until they are able to actually master it. They crave flattery, and prefer women who comply and cater to them. Leos demand unconditional obedience, and constant approval. When a Leo is in love, he is fairly sexual, and capable of being devoted and faithful. Cheap love affairs are not his thing, and Leos are highly aware of how expensive it is to divorce. They make excellent fathers. A Leo's partner needs to look polished and well-dressed, and he will not tolerate either frumpiness or nerds.

Aries, Sagittarius, and Gemini make for good matches. Leos are often very beguiling to Libras; this is the most infamous astrological "master-slave" pairing. Leos are also inexplicably drawn to Pisces – this is the only sign capable of taming them. A Leo and Virgo will face a host of problems sooner or later, and they might be material in nature. The Virgo will attempt to conquer him, and if she does, a breakup is inevitable.

VIRGO

Virgo is a highly intellectual sign, who likes to take a step back and spend his time studying the big picture. But love inherently does not lend itself to analysis, and this can leave Virgos feeling perplexed. While Virgo is taking his time, studying the object of his affection, someone else will swoop in and take her away, leaving him bitterly disappointed. Perhaps for that reason, Virgos tend to marry late, but once they are married, they remain true, and hardly ever initiate divorce. In bed, they are modest and reserved, as they see sex as some sort of quirk of nature, designed solely for procreation. Most Virgos have a gifted sense of taste, hearing, and smell. They cannot tolerate pungent odors and can be squeamish; they believe their partners should always take pains to be very clean. Virgos usually hate over-the-top expressions of love, and are immune to sex as a mean s of control. Many Virgos are stingy and more appropriate as husbands than lovers. Male Virgos tend to be monogamous, though if they are unhappy or disappointed with their partner, they may begin to look for comfort elsewhere and often give in to drunkenness.

Taurus, Capricorn, and Scorpio make the best partners for a Virgo. They may feel inexplicable attraction for Aquarians. They will form friendships with Aries, but rarely will this couple make it down the aisle. With Leos, be careful – this sign is best as a lover, not a spouse.

LIBRA

Libra is a very complex, wishy-washy sign. They are constantly seeking perfection, which often leaves them in discord with the reality around them. Libra men are elegant and refined, and expect no less from their partner. Many Libras treat their partners like a beautiful work of art, and have trouble holding onto the object of their affection. They view love itself as a very abstract concept, and can get tired of the physical aspect of their relationship. They are much more drawn to intrigue and the chase- dreams, candlelit evenings, and other symbols of romance. A high percentage of Libra men are gay, and they view sex with other men as the more elite option. Even when Libras are unhappy in their marriages, they never divorce willingly. Their wives might leave them, however, or they might be taken away by a more decisive partner.

Aquarius and Gemini make the best matches for Libras. Libra can also easily control an independent Sagittarius, and can easily fall under the influence of a powerful and determined Leo, before putting all his strength and effort into breaking free. Relationships with Scorpios are difficult; they may become lovers, but will rarely marry.

SCORPIO

Though it is common to perceive Scorpios as incredibly sexual, they are, in fact, very unassuming, and never brag about their exploits. They will, however, be faithful and devoted to the right woman. The Scorpio man is taciturn, and you can't expect any tender words from him, but he will defend those he loves to the very end. Despite his outward control, Scorpio is very emotional; he needs and craves love, and is willing to fight for it. Scorpios are incredible lovers, and rather than leaving them tired, sex leaves them feeling energized. They are always sexy, even if they aren't particularly handsome. They are unconcerned with the ceremony of wooing you, and more focused on the act of love itself.

Expressive Cancers and gentle, amenable Pisces make the best partners. A Scorpio might also fall under the spell of a Virgo, who is adept at taking the lead. Sparks might fly between two Scorpios, or with a Taurus, who is perfect for a Scorpio in bed. Relationships with Libras, Sagittarians, and Aries are difficult.

SAGITTARIUS

Sagittarian men are lucky, curious, and gregarious. Younger Sagittarians are romantic, passionate, and burning with desire to experience every type of love. Sagittarius is a very idealistic sign, and in that search for perfection, they tend to flit from one partner to another, eventually forgetting what they were even looking for in the first place. A negative Sagittarius might have two or three relationships going on at once, assigning each partner a different day of the week. On the other hand, a positive Sagittarius will channel his powerful sexual energy into creativity, and take his career to new heights. Generally speaking, after multiple relationships and divorces, the Sagittarian man will conclude that his ideal marriage is one where his partner is willing to look the other way.

Aries and Leo make the best matches for a Sagittarius. He might fall under the spell of a Cancer, but would not be happy being married to her. Gemini can be very intriguing, but will only make for a happy marriage after middle age, when both partners are older and wiser. Younger Sagittarians often marry Aquarian women, but things quickly fall apart. Scorpios can make for an interesting relationship, but if the Sagittarius fails to comply, divorce is inevitable.

CAPRICORN

Practical, reserved Capricorn is one of the least sexual signs of the Zodiac. He views sex as an idle way to pass the time, and something he can live without, until he wants to start a family. He tends to marry late, and almost never divorces. Young Capricorns are prone to suppressing their sexual desires, and only discover them later in life, when they have already achieved everything a real man needs – a career and money. We'll be frank – Capricorn is not the best lover, but he can compensate by being caring, attentive, and showering you with valuable gifts. Ever cautious, Capricorn loves to schedule his sexual relationships, and this is something partners will just have to accept. Women should understand that Capricorn needs some help relaxing – perhaps with alcohol. They prefer inconspicuous, unassuming women, and run away from a fashion plate.

The best partners for a Capricorn are Virgo, Taurus, or Scorpio. Cancers might catch his attention, and if they marry, it is likely to be for life. Capricorn is able to easily dominate Pisces, and Pisces-Capricorn is a well-known "slave and master" combination. Relationships with Leos tend to be erratic, and they are unlikely to wed. Aries might make for a cozy family at first, but things will cool off quickly, and often, the marriage only lasts as long as Capricorn is unwilling to make a change in his life.

AQUARIUS

Aquarian men are mercurial, and often come off as peculiar, unusual, or aloof, and detached. Aquarians are turned on by anything novel or strange, and they are constantly looking for new and interesting people. They are stimulated by having a variety of sexual partners, but they consider this to simply be normal life, rather than sexually immoral. Aquarians are unique – they are more abstract than realistic, and can be cold and incomprehensible, even in close relationships. Once an Aquarius gets married, he will try to remain within the realm of decency, but often fails. An Aquarian's partners need uncommon patience, as nothing they do can restrain him. Occasionally, one might encounter another kind of Aquarius – a responsible, hard worker, and exemplary family man.

The best matches for an Aquarius are female fellow Aquarians, Libras, and Sagittarians. When Aquarius seeks out yet another affair, he is not choosy, and will be happy with anyone.

PISCES

Pisces is the most eccentric sign of the Zodiac. This is reflected in his romantic tendencies and sex life. Pisces men become very dependent on those with whom they have a close relationship. Paradoxically, they are simultaneously crafty and childlike when it comes to playing games, and they are easily deceived. As a double bodied sign, Pisces rarely marry just once, as they are very sexual, easily fall in love, and are constantly seeking their ideal. Pisces are very warm people, who love to take care of others and are inclined toward "slave-master" relationships, in which they are the submissive partner. But after catering to so many lovers, Pisces will remain elusive. They are impossible to figure out ahead of time – today, they might be declaring their love for you, but tomorrow, they may disappear – possibly forever! To a Pisces, love is a fantasy, illusion, and dream, and they might spend their whole lives in pursuit of it. Pisces who are unhappy in love are vulnerable to alcoholism or drug addiction.

Cancer and Scorpio make the best partners for a Pisces. He is also easily dominated by Capricorn and Libra, but in turn will conquer even a queen-like Leo. Often, they are fascinated by Geminis – if they marry, it will last a long time, but likely not forever. Relationships with Aries and Sagittarians are erratic, though initially, things can seem almost perfect.

Women

ARIES

Aries women are leaders. They are decisive, bold, and very protective. An Aries can take initiative and is not afraid to make the first move. Her ideal man is strong, and someone she can admire. But remember, at the slightest whiff of weakness, she will knock him off his pedestal. She does not like dull, whiny men, and thinks that there is always a way out of any situation. If she loves someone, she will be faithful. Aries women are too honest to try leading a double life. They are possessive, jealous, and not only will they not forgive those who are unfaithful, their revenge may be brutal; they know no limits. If you can handle an Aries, don't try to put her in a cage; it is best to give her a long leash. Periodically give her some space – then she will seek you out herself. She is sexual, and believe that anything goes in bed.

Her best partners are a Sagittarius or Leo. A Libra can make a good match after middle age, once both partners have grown wiser and settled down a bit. Gemini and Aquarius are only good partners during the initial phase, when everything is still new, but soon enough, they will lose interest in each other. Scorpios are good matches in bed, but only suitable as lovers.

TAURUS

Taurean women possess qualities that men often dream about, but rarely find in the flesh – they are soft, charming, practical, and reliable – they are very caring and will support their partner in every way. A Taurus is highly sexual, affectionate, and can show a man how to take pleasure to new heights. She is also strong and intense. If she is in love, she will be faithful. But when love fades away, she might find someone else on the side, though she will still fight to save her marriage, particularly if her husband earns good money. A Taurus will not tolerate a man who is disheveled or disorganized, and anyone dating her needs to always be on his toes. She will expect gifts, and likes being taken to expensive restaurants, concerts, and other events. If you argue, try to make the first peace offering, because a Taurus finds it very hard to do so – she might withdraw and ruminate for a long time. Never air your dirty laundry; solve all your problems one-on-one.

Scorpio, Virgo, Capricorn, and Cancer make the best matches. A relationship with an Aries or Sagittarius would be difficult. There is little attraction between a Taurus and a Leo, and initially Libras can make for a good partner in bed, but things will quickly cool off and fall apart. A Taurus and Aquarius make an interesting match – despite the difference in signs, their relationships are often lasting, and almost lifelong.

GEMINI

Gemini women are social butterflies, outgoing, and they easily make friends, and then break off the friendship, if people do not hold their interest. A Gemini falls in love hard, is very creative, and often fantasizes about the object of her affection. She is uninterested in sex without any attachment, loves to flirt, and, for the most part, is not particularly affectionate. She dreams of a partner who is her friend, lover, and a romantic, all at once. A Gemini has no use for a man who brings nothing to the table intellectually. That is a tall order, so Geminis often divorce and marry several times. Others simply marry later in life. Once you have begun a life together, do not try to keep her inside – she needs to travel, explore, socialize, attend events and go to the theater. She cannot tolerate possessive men, so avoid giving her the third degree, and remember that despite her flirtatious and social nature, she is, in fact, faithful – as long as you keep her interested and she is in love. Astrologists believe that Geminis do not know what they need until age 29 or 30, so it is best to hold off on marriage until then.

Leo and Libra make the best matches. A relationship with a Cancer is likely, though complex, and depends solely on the Cancer's affection. A Gemini and Sagittarius can have an interesting, dynamic relationship, but these are two restless signs, which might only manage to get together after ages 40-45, once they have had enough thrills out of life and learned to be patient. Relationships with a Capricorn are very difficult, and almost never happen. The honeymoon stage can be wonderful with a Scorpio, but each partner will eventually go their own way, before ending things. A Gemini and Pisces union can also be very interesting – they are drawn to each other, and can have a wonderful relationship, but after a while, the cracks start to show and things will fall apart. An Aquarius is also not a bad match, but they will have little sexual chemistry.

CANCER

Cancers can be divided into two opposing groups. The first includes a sweet and gentle creature who is willing to dedicate her life to her husband and children. She is endlessly devoted to her husband, especially if he makes a decent living and remains faithful. She views all men as potential husbands, which means it is dangerous to strike up a relationship with her if your intentions are not serious; she can be anxious and clingy, sensitive and prone to crying. It is better to break things to her gently, rather than directly spitting out the cold, hard truth. She wants a man who can be a provider, though she often earns well herself. She puts money away for a rainy day, and knows how to be thrifty, for the sake of others around her, rather than only for herself. She is an excellent cook and capable of building an inviting home for her loved ones. She is enthusiastic in bed, a wonderful wife, and a caring mother.

The second type of Cancer is neurotic, and capable of creating a living hell for those around her. She believes that the world is her enemy, and manages to constantly find new intrigue and machinations.

Another Cancer, Virgo, Taurus, Scorpio, and Pisces make the best matches. A Cancer can often fall in love with a Gemini, but eventually, things will grow complicated, as she will be exhausted by a Gemini's constant mood swings and cheating. A Cancer and Sagittarius will initially have passionate sex, but things will quickly cool off. A relationship with a Capricorn is a real possibility, but only later in life, as while they are young, they are likely to fight and argue constantly.

Cancer can also have a relationship with an Aries, but this will not be easy.

LEO

Leos are usually beautiful or charming, and outwardly sexual. And yet, appearances can be deceiving – they are not actually that interested in sex. Leo women want to be the center of attention and men running after them boosts their self-esteem, but they are more interested in their career, creating something new, and success than sex. They often have high-powered careers and are proud of their own achievements. Their partners need to be strong; if a Leo feels a man is weak, she can carry him herself for a while- before leaving him. It is difficult for her to find a partner for life, as chivalrous knights are a dying breed, and she is not willing to compromise. If you are interested in a Leo, take the initiative, admire her, and remember that even a queen is still a woman. Timid men or tightwads need not apply. Leos like to help others, but they don't need a walking disaster in their life. If they are married and in love, they are usually faithful, and petty gossip isn't their thing. Leo women make excellent mothers, and are ready to give their lives to their children. Their negative traits include vanity and a willingness to lie, in order to make themselves look better.

Sagittarius, Aries, and Libra make the best matches. Leos can also have an interesting relationship with a Virgo, though both partners will weaken each other. Life with a Taurus will lead to endless arguments – both signs are very stubborn, and unwilling to give in. Leos and Pisces are another difficult pair, as she will have to learn to be submissive if she wants to keep him around. A relationship with a Capricorn will work if there is a common denominator, but they will have little sexual chemistry. Life with a Scorpio will be turbulent to say the least, and they will usually break up later in life.

VIRGO

Virgo women are practical, clever, and often duplicitous. Marrying one isn't for everyone. She is a neat freak to the point of annoying those around her. She is also an excellent cook, and strives to ensure her children receive the very best by teaching them everything, and preparing them for a bright future. She is also thrifty – she won't throw money around, and, in fact, won't even give it to her husband. She has no time for rude, macho strongmen, and is suspicious of spendthrifts. She will not be offended if you take her to a cozy and modest café rather than an elegant restaurant. Virgos are masters of intrigue, and manage to outperform every other sign of the Zodiac in this regard. Virgos love to criticize everyone and everything; to listen to them, the entire world is simply a disaster and wrong, and only she is the exception to this rule. Virgos are not believed to be particularly sexual, but there are different variations when it comes to this. Rarely, one finds an open-minded Virgo willing to try anything, and who does it all on a grand scale – but she is rather the exception to this general rule.

The best matches for a Virgo are Cancer, Taurus, and Capricorn. She also can get along well with a Scorpio, but will find conflict with Sagittarius. A Pisces will strike her interest, but they will rarely make it down the aisle. She is often attracted to an Aquarius, but they would drive each other up the wall were they to actually marry. An Aries forces Virgo to see another side of life, but here, she will have to learn to conform and adapt.

LIBRA

Female Libras tend to be beautiful, glamorous, or very charming. They are practical, tactical, rational, though they are adept at hiding these qualities behind their romantic and elegant appearance. Libras are drawn to marriage, and are good at imagining the kind of partner they need. They seek out strong, well-off men and are often more interested in someone's social status and bank account than feelings. The object of their affection needs to be dashing, and have a good reputation in society. Libras love expensive things, jewelry, and finery. If they are feeling down, a beautiful gift will instantly cheer them up. They will not tolerate scandal or conflict, and will spend all their energy trying to keep the peace, or at least the appearance thereof. They do not like to air their dirty laundry, and will only divorce in extreme circumstances. They are always convinced they are right and react to any objections as though they have been insulted. Most Libras are not particularly sexual, except those with Venus or the Moon in Scorpio.

Leos, Geminis, and Aquarians make good matches. Libra women are highly attracted to Aries men - this is a real case of opposites attract. They can get along with a Sagittarius, though he will find that Libras are too proper and calm. Capricorn, Pisces, and Cancer are all difficult matches. Things will begin tumultuously with a Taurus, before each partner goes his or her own way.

SCORPIO

Scorpio women may appear outwardly restrained, but there is much more bubbling below the surface. They are ambitious with high self-esteem, but often wear a mask of unpretentiousness. They are the true power behind the scenes, the one who holds the family together, but never talk about it. Scorpios are strong-willed, resilient, and natural survivors. Often, Scorpios are brutally honest, and expect the same out of those around them. They do not like having to conform, and attempt to get others to adapt to them, as they honestly believe everyone will be better off that way. They are incredibly intuitive, and not easily deceived. They have an excellent memory, and can quickly figure out which of your buttons to push. They are passionate in bed, and their temperament will not diminish with age. When she is sexually frustrated, a Scorpio will throw all of her energy into her career or her loved ones. She is proud, categorical, and "if you don't do it right, don't do it at all" is her motto. Scorpio cannot be fooled, and she will not forgive any cheating. Will she cheat herself? Yes! But it will not break up her family, and she will attempt to keep it a secret. Scorpios are usually attractive to men, even if they are not particularly beautiful. They keep a low profile, though they always figure out their partner, and give them some invisible sign. There is also another, selfish type of Scorpio, who will use others for as long as they need them, before unceremoniously casting them aside.

Taurus is a good match; they will have excellent sexual chemistry and understand each other. Scorpio and Gemini are drawn to each other, but are unlikely to stay together long enough to actually get married. Cancer can be a good partner as well, but Cancers are possessive, while Scorpios do not like others meddling in their affairs, though they can later resolve their arguments in bed. Scorpio and Leo are often found together, but their relationship can also be very complicated. Leos are animated and chipper, while Scorpios, who are much deeper and more stubborn, see Leos as not particularly serious or reliable. One good example of this is Bill (a Leo) and Hillary (a Scorpio) Clinton. Virgo can also make a good partner, but when Scorpio seemingly lacks emotions, he will look for them elsewhere. Relationships with Lira are strange and very rare. Scorpio sees Libra as too insecure, and Libra does not appreciate Scorpio's rigidity. Two Scorpios together make an excellent marriage! Sagittarius and Scorpio are unlikely to get together, as she will think he is shallow and rude. If they do manage to get married, Scorpio's drive and persistence is the only thing that will make the marriage last. Capricorn is also not a bad match, and while Scorpio finds Aquarius attractive, they will rarely get married, as they are simply speaking different languages! Things are alright with a Pisces, as both signs are emotional, and Pisces can let Scorpio take the lead when necessary.

SAGITTARIUS

Sagittarius women are usually charming, bubbly, energetic, and have the gift of gab. They are kind, sincere, and love people. They are also straightforward, fair, and very ambitious, occasionally to the point of irritating those around them. But telling them something is easier than not telling them, and they often manage to win over their enemies. Sagittarius tends to have excellent intuition, and she loves to both learn and teach others. She is a natural leader, and loves taking charge at work and at home. Many Sagittarian women have itchy feet, and prefer all kinds of travel to sitting at home. They are not particularly good housewives – to be frank, cooking and cleaning is simply not for them. Their loved ones must learn to adapt to them, but Sagittarians themselves hate any pressure. They are not easy for men to handle, as Sagittarians want to be in charge. Sagittarius falls in love easily, is very sexual and temperamental, and may marry multiple times. Despite outward appearances, Sagittarius is a very lonely sign. Even after she is married with children, she may continue living as if she were alone; you might say she marches to the beat of her own drum. Younger Sagittarians can be reckless, but as they mature, they can be drawn to religion, philosophy, and the occult.

Aries and Leo make the best matches, as Sagittarius is able to bend to Leo's ways, or at least pretend to. Sagittarians often end up with Aquarians, but their marriages do not tend to be for the long haul. They are attracted to Geminis, but are unlikely to marry one until middle age, when both signs have settled down. Sagittarius and Cancer have incredible sexual chemistry, but an actual relationship between them would be tumultuous and difficult. Capricorn can make a good partner-as long as they are able to respect each other's quirks. Sagittarius rarely ends up with a Virgo, and while she may often meet Pisces, things are unlikely to go very far.

CAPRICORN

Capricorn women are conscientious, reliable, organized, and hard-working. Many believe that life means nothing but work, and live accordingly. They are practical, and not particularly drawn to parties or loud groups of people. But if someone useful will be there, they are sure to make an appearance. Capricorn women are stingy, but not as much as their male counterparts. They are critical of others, but think highly of themselves. Generally, they take a difficult path in life, but thanks to their dedication, perseverance, and willingness to push their own limits, they are able to forge their own path, and by 45 or 50, they can provide themselves with anything they could want. Capricorn women have the peculiarity of looking older than their peers when they are young, and younger than everyone else once they have matured. They are not particularly sexual, and tend to be faithful partners. They rarely divorce, and even will fight until the end, even for a failed marriage. Many Capricorns have a pessimistic outlook of life, and have a tendency to be depressed. They are rarely at the center of any social circle, but are excellent organizers. They have a very rigid view of life and love, and are not interested in a fling, as marriage is the end goal. As a wife, Capricorn is simultaneously difficult and reliable. She is difficult because of her strict nature and difficulty adapting. But she will also take on all the household duties, and her husband can relax, knowing his children are in good hands.

Taurus, Pisces, and Scorpio make good matches. Aries is difficult, once things cool off after the initial honeymoon. When a Capricorn meets another Capricorn, they will be each other's first and last love. Sagittarius isn't a bad match, but they don't always pass the test of time. Aquarius and Capricorn are a difficult match, and rarely found together. Things are too dull with a Virgo, and while Leo can be exciting at first, things will fall apart when he begins showing off. Libra and Aquarius are both difficult partners for Capricorn, and she is rarely found with either of them.

AQUARIUS

A female Aquarius is very different from her male counterparts. She is calm and keeps a cool head, but she is also affectionate and open. She values loyalty above all else, and is unlikely to recover from any infidelity, though she will only divorce if this becomes a chronic trend, and she has truly been stabbed in the back. She is not interested in her partner's money, but rather, his professional success. She is unobtrusive and trusting, and will refrain from listening in on her partner's phone conversations or hacking into his email. With rare exceptions, Aquarian women make terrible housewives. But they are excellent partners in life – they are faithful, never boring, and will not reject a man, even in the most difficult circumstances. Most Aquarians are highly intuitive, and can easily tell the truth from a lie. They themselves only lie in extreme situations, which call for a "white lie" in order to avoid hurting someone's feelings.

Aquarius gets along well with Aries, Gemini, and Libra. She can also have a good relationship with a Sagittarius. Taurus often makes a successful match, though they are emotionally very different; the same goes for

Virgo. Aquarius and Scorpio, Capricorn, or Cancer is a difficult match. Pisces can make a good partner as well, as both signs complement each other. Any relationship with a Leo will be tumultuous, but lasting, as Leo is selfish, and Aquarius will therefore have to be very forgiving.

PISCES

Pisces women are very adaptable, musically inclined, and erotic. They possess an innate earthly wisdom, and a good business sense. Pisces often reinvent themselves; they can be emotional, soft, and obstinate, as well as sentimental, at times. Their behavioral changes can be explained by frequent ups and downs. Pisces is charming, caring, and her outward malleability is very attractive to men. She is capable of loving selflessly, as long as the man has something to love. Even if he doesn't, she will try and take care of him until the very end. Pisces' greatest fear is poverty. They are intuitive, vulnerable, and always try to avoid conflict. They love to embellish the truth, and sometimes alcohol helps with this. Rarely, one finds extremely unbalanced, neurotic and dishonest Pisces, who are capable of turning their loved ones' lives into a living Hell!

Taurus, Capricorn, Cancer, and Scorpio make the best matches. She will be greatly attracted to a Virgo, but a lasting relationship is only likely if both partners are highly spiritual. Any union with a Libra is likely to be difficult and full of conflict. Pisces finds Gemini attractive, and they may have a very lively relationship – for a while. Occasionally, Pisces ends up with a Sagittarius, but she will have to fade into the background and entirely submit to him. If she ends up with an Aquarius, expect strong emotional outbursts, and a marriage that revolves around the need to raise their children.

Tatiana Borsch

Printed in Great Britain
by Amazon

33099035R00062